I0811043

Wearing a Broken Indigene Heart on the Sleeve of Christian Mission

Wearing a Broken Indigene Heart on the Sleeve of Christian Mission

Carmen Lansdowne

CMU PRESS
WINNIPEG, MANITOBA
2025

CMU PRESS

CMU Press
Canadian Mennonite University
500 Shaftesbury Blvd.
Winnipeg MB R3P2N2
www.cmupress.ca

CMU Press is learning and striving to create an inclusive and welcoming space for people of many identities and communities. We work on land which is the ancestral home of the Anishinaabe, Cree, Dakota, and Métis peoples. We are grateful for their stewardship of this place.

Editor: Josiah Neufeld
Copyeditor: Sue Sorensen
Cover designer: Jonathan Dyck
Layout designer: Galley Creative Co.
Editorial assistants: Phil Waldner, Logan Nord, Emma Siemens
Endpaper art by Katie Anderson
Cover art: Patricia June Vickers, Bits and Pieces No. 17, mixed media on watercolour paper

Printed in Canada by Hignell Book Printing, Winnipeg.

ISBN 978-1-987986-18-1

MIX
Paper | Supporting responsible forestry
FSC www.fsc.org
FSC® C013916

Some of the material from chapter five appears in a slightly different form in "It Is a Strict Law That Bids Us Dance: Kwakwa̱ka̱'wakw and Haíłzaqv Transforming Christianity by Receiving the 'Other'" within *Decolonizing Church: Emerging Voices Speak,* edited by Néstor Medina and Becca Whitla.

Library and Archives Canada Cataloguing in Publication

Title: Wearing a broken Indigene heart on the sleeve of Christian mission / Carmen Lansdowne.
Names: Lansdowne, Carmen, author.
Description: Includes bibliographical references.
Identifiers: Canadiana 20250227231 | ISBN 9781987986181 (softcover)
Subjects: LCSH: Missions—Canada. | LCSH: Indigenous peoples—Missions—Canada. | LCSH: Indigenous peoples—Canada—Religion. | CSH: Church work with Indigenous peoples—Canada.
Classification: LCC BV2810 .L36 2025 | DDC 266.0089/97071—dc23

Contents

To my family—

To my children Gabriel & Esperanza
who remind me to be a messenger of hope,

to my husband Mauricio who always has my back—"so much,"

to my brother Robb for inspiring me—I love all that you do and are,

to my parents: dad—for all your advice, encouragements, and listening,

and especially my mother—above all others—
without your teaching and influence I wouldn't have these thoughts.

Acknowledgements

SO MANY PEOPLE have participated in the genesis of this book. First and foremost, I must thank my family for their support, encouragement, understanding, patience, impatience, and belief that I could do this and that the voice I add to the academy adds value. My children have suffered periods of absence and distraction, but I hope have also been profoundly shaped by my theology. My partner, Mauricio, has borne the brunt of the mundane household chores and parenting duties while I stretched myself—often too thinly—between work, study, and other leadership commitments. I am absolutely convinced that I could not have done this without him. One of my greatest joys early in my studies was falling in love with him in Bay Area coffee shops while we read theology and philosophy together—thanks to a broken ankle and him being off work for a significant number of months. For many years the busyness of life limited our ability to engage in these deeper discussions, but our life together is undergirded by the visions we share for the world and why theology is important. I'm deeply grateful in this current phase of life and with my current writing projects that those conversations are sprouting anew after long years lying fallow in the field. He will never be able to convince me, despite his protests to the contrary, that priests and theologians are useless sons of bitches. However, the fact that we both believe that too often this has been the case is in large part what inspires me to be both a priest and theologian who matters and whose words and actions are useful.

There are no words to thank my parents. To try and put words to paper that express my gratitude simply reduces me to tears. They are the embodiment of unconditional love and grace. I owe them everything.

To my doctoral committee: Philip Wickeri, my advisor, for redirecting my efforts from Israel Palestine back to where they belong, focused on my own experience and passions, and for guiding me from a distance, in Hong Kong, as his vocation drew him away from the Graduate Theological Union (GTU). Eddie Fernández, also of the GTU, was a delight to think through mission with, and his insistent *joie de vivre* is contagious. When I think of the hopefulness of the Christian faith, Eddie's face comes to mind. Tom Biolsi of UC Berkeley was an encouragement since my first semester at the GTU. He introduced me to much of the canon of race and ethnic studies and gave me a place to think through theological intersections with the wider academy. I appreciated his gentle curiosity about this proposed Indigenous theology and his interest in my work. And to Jenny Plane Te Paa, my Indigenous auntie and Māori mother in the academy, for instructing me pre-PhD that she *would* be on my committee when it came time, and for always being there. For understanding the shared experiences of trying to do too much and being called on by the church in ways that made the completion of my dissertation and then this book seem almost impossible for much of the time. For leaving a trail for me to follow through the desert of doctoral studies and proving that you can be a mother, a church leader, a theologian, and work-full time while writing. You made me believe I could do it, even when others wished I could or would do it a different way.

The Rev. Dr. Sharon Betcher is the reason I had the confidence to pursue doctoral studies in theology and has been an unwavering champion. I would not have finished without her thoughts in addition to Philip's. Ines Backes, our *au pair* during finalization of my writing, for her support in watching the kids so I could write. To colleagues Joerg Rieger, Karen Hamilton, Rob Fennell, Ross Lockhart, Jayakiran Sebastian, Robert O. Smith, Claudio Carvalhaes, and Hyuk Cho for your willingness to pre-read and endorse my book.

John Boopalan made the introduction to Sue Sorensen, editor at CMU Press, who agreed to publish this book. Sue, in turn, and recognizing my plate was full (overfull?) as I served a term as Moderator of The United Church of Canada, hired Josiah Neufeld as additional editorial support. I've learned to become a better writer because of his keen eye and kind suggestions of how I could say things more simply. And to Patricia J. Vickers, Indigenous scholar, practitioner, and artist: thank you for agreeing to let me use "Bits and Pieces #17" as the cover art for this book.

Lastly, I want to acknowledge all the theologians and church leaders with whom I've crossed paths during the past fifteen years and more who have inspired and encouraged me, my community and my inspiration. In no particular order: Tink Tinker, Teresa Burnett-Cole, Cheryl Bear, Nancy Cardoso Pereira, Ofelia Ortega, Santiago Slabodsky, Marion Grau, Richard Leggett, Stan McKay, Norah McMurtry, Edwin Searcy, Janet Gear, Elaine Nogueira-Godsey, John Thatamanil, Thia Cooper (thank you for translating Dussel you glorious woman!), Devin Singh, Michael Blair, Michelle Voss, Nestor Medina, Matthew Gaudet, Patricia Dutcher Walls, Harry O. Maier, Jim Lindenburger, Brian Thorpe, Olav Fykse Tveit, Guillermo Kerber, Archbishop Vicken Aykazian, Paula Der Matoian, Yusef Daher, Mitri Raheb, Viola Raheb, Wendy Arce, Christine Boyle, Graham Brownmiller, Ingrid Hartloff Brown, Danielle Ayana James, Michael Shewberg, Jennifer Goddard-Shepard, David Giuliano, Peter Short, Treena Duncan, Don Robertson, Deb Bowman, Jamie Scott, Rob Dalgleish, Rachel Haxtema, Kwame Assenyoh, Nicanor Sarmiento, Marco Murillo, Glenys Huws, Harry Oussoren, Bishop Owdenburg Mdegella, the late Sallie McFague, the late Cliff McMurtry, the late Maria Chavez, the late Ibrahim Farajaje, and the late Christopher Lind. Conversations and experiences with all of you are woven through this work.

Preface

I speak of a private need
To feel part of a shifting public
To be seen by other brown eyes
Sometimes blue or grey or green
Eyes that are slowly taking back
What was
And is
At the root
Of what always has been

I am because I have come to be
Unformed braids
Hit my shoulders awkwardly
Half-formed opinions
Half-bred blood and DNA

—*Kinnie Starr, "Rifles"*[1]

THIS BOOK IS very much a labour of love, which is fitting coming from a Christian missiologist. I have written from a place of deep commitment to and love for the Christian faith. As an Indigenous woman, I have been asked many times, from both inside and outside the church, why I choose to be Christian at all. Grappling with the answer has led me down a winding path in my scholarship: from not being able to clearly state my voice, to focusing too much on my own emotional reality and avoiding the rigorous scholarly work I enjoy about being a scholar. Hopefully the work I have started here lands somewhere in a healthy middle.

A personal story

I have an acute memory of getting feedback on a paper I wrote for a course I took during my second theological degree. It was my first real attempt to theorize theologically about the way my ministry and global experience were playing out in my life, and I argued for the value of cosmopolitanism, especially from my experience as a very well-travelled young Indigenous theologian. I was quite excited about the way my thoughts had taken shape in the paper. I struggled with the course in general, so finding a concept I could explore with enthusiasm was a lifesaver. I expected that my professor would be as excited as I was about what I was trying to express. But rather than the glowing accolades I was expecting, I received what felt like rejection (I'm sure she did not intend as such). Her comments were something to the effect of "this type of Hegelian universalism has been thoroughly critiqued in the academy."

I had not intended to put forward a universalizing view in line with the worst of Western hegemonic theology and philosophy; I had merely explained how my experience had helped me to find commonalities in the experience of the world's majority poor and oppressed through the opportunity to travel globally for different meetings and consultations with the World Council of Churches. Why could my professor not understand what I was trying to say? The question baffled me for years.

It was not until I started to delve more deeply into philosophy and liberation theologies that I began to understand my professor's critique and to gain more clarity about where I wanted to position myself as a scholar.

I'd grown up being told by non-Indigenous people in the church that the reason liberation theology hadn't worked for Indigenous Peoples in *Kanata* was because we lacked the critical population mass of the economic poor of Latin America or the Black majority under Apartheid South Africa. At the time of my professor's rebuke, I was still developing my own scholarly voice, and I was not confident enough to disagree with her. On the surface, her comments made logical sense. There *are* extra challenges to asserting Indigenous Rights when you only make up three or four percent of the population. When I began to seriously engage with liberationists, I approached them from the perspective I had learned: that liberation theology and pedagogies of the oppressed had failed my people. Very quickly I came to see that it was not liberation theology that had failed my people, but rather, the church had failed liberation theology.

For example, in the early 1980s The United Church of Canada created a series of Indigenous theological training programs. One of the schools, then called the Dr. Jessie Saulteaux Centre, was supposedly built on the community model of learning that Paulo Freire presented in *Pedagogy of the Oppressed*.[2] Freire advocated models of transformational community-based learning in which those who had been made marginal incorporated their lived experience as a lens for making sense of, and critiquing, the systems that oppressed them. Rather than offering the eight- or nine-month annual residential programs for MDiv students that were standard at theological schools at the time, the Centre focused primarily on community-based learning. Candidates for ministry would come together at the Centre for two-week learning circles four times a year. The remainder of their learning was supposed to be done while practising ministry in their home communities. In theory, the program is supposed to be praxis-based, with time for critical reflection and transformation during learning circles. In practice, however, for many years the church set up the model but missed out on the intended outcome of conscientization, or critical consciousness. It was community-based learning, but not always *transformational* community. The learning circles (depending on leadership and faculty) often provided a sub standard theological education that mirrored a watered-down version of the more robust MDiv sought by non-Indigenous students who go to "real" seminaries. Having taught at the school off and on since 2009 and having served on its board of directors, I am certain that the program, even after thirty years, is still partially void of the awakening consciousness that marked true critical Freirean pedagogy.

After years of struggling against that blinkered mislabel, "Hegelian universalism," I finally found my answer as I started to work my way through Enrique Dussel's *Politics of Liberation*. In her translator's preface, Thia Cooper points out that "For Dussel, the key to a politics of liberation is first to read history with a 'global' and 'decolonized' lens; only then can the task of political liberation begin."[3] When one reads history with a global and decolonized lens, one begins to see the commonalities among those living on the underside of modernity.[4] This is what I was trying to say in that ill-fated paper. History has consistently shown us how divide and conquer is used as a strategy of oppression. So, for me to claim a seat at the table of the oppressed was an important anti-colonial act.

In the first part of *Politics of Liberation*, Dussel writes:

> The critical discourse of liberation . . . has to abandon the fragmentation of its story and produce a critical macro-story with the claim of truth (that is to say, aware that it is inevitably fallible, but still advanced as a truth claim) in order for the imagined victims, those dominated, to have the capacity to protect itself in a historical place with meaning, with global meaning (which will have to be corrected; therefore the macro-story is inevitably fallible).[5]

The global macro-story becomes a safe place for those who have been made marginal. In other words, although each situation of oppression and colonization is distinct, the work of studying the effects of colonization and oppression in different contexts globally can create an affinity among those who experience it, and gives voice to a common struggle. This is not to discount the value of situating oneself as a scholar within a particular social or theological location. Writing at a more theoretical "macro-story" level does not in any way detract from my Indigeneity, rather it aligns the experiences of the *Haíłzaqv* people with the oppression experienced by tribal peoples in India or South Africans under Apartheid, and myriad others.

As is argued elsewhere, theological scholarship can be used both to oppress and to liberate.[6] Words are double-edged swords that need context and clarification. In the epistles, the apostle Paul's famous words "There is no longer Jew nor Greek, there is no longer slave nor free, there is no longer male and female; for all of you are one in Christ Jesus" (Galatians 3.28), could be read by Settler and Arrivant societies in North America as endorsing the colonization (or at least the normativity of colonial history) of Indigenous Peoples. What I mean is this: The dominant sectors in society like to disconnect the harms of the past from our political present. "Why don't Indigenous people get over the past and pull themselves up by their bootstraps and make a better life for themselves? We're all just ______ [read: Canadian / American / European / Latine, etc.]." These rhetorical tactics support a Settler mentality that sees itself disconnected from the conquest of the whole of America (for North, Central, and South are one continent). These tactics say that because we are all equal, therefore we all have equal opportunity. However, an Indigenist[7] reading of Galatians 3.28, as a reading from the underside of modernity, calls to account biblical interpretation that sanitizes the politics of oppression.

I feel it is important to conclude this preface with a personal story of how theological "truths" have touched me as a scholar and as a person of faith. My brother is a therapist who used the emerging discipline of autoethnography as the primary methodology of his scholarly work. Autoethnography is "research, writing, story, and method that connect the autobiographical and personal to the cultural, social, and political."[8]

Autoethnography is an emergent field not well known in theological circles, which is why I choose not to employ it explicitly as a method throughout this book. That said, I do believe in its importance to Indigenous scholars because it helps to make the truth (or, more accurately, *our truths*) of Indigenous political struggles more tangible. Tactics in autoethnography are to write therapeutically, vulnerably, evocatively, and ethically.[9] Ruth Behar, an anthropologist who uses autobiographical methods in her work, writes about the vulnerability of using the personal narrative as method. She states, "Vulnerability doesn't mean that anything personal goes. The exposure of the self who is also a spectator must take us somewhere we otherwise wouldn't get to. It must be essential to the argument, not a decorative flourish, not exposure for its own sake."[10] While I do make myself vulnerable in certain explicit and implicit ways in this book, it is not something I do consistently.

Rather than employ autoethnographic methods throughout, I prefer simply to end this preface with a personal narrative. When I wrote my PhD dissertation that eventually became this book, the original title was "Bearing Witness: Wearing a Broken Indigene Heart on the Sleeve of the *Missio Dei*." I wanted to bear witness by sharing the multitude of ways that the church has broken my heart, and why I still believe there is cause for faith, hope, and love through the religious vehicle of Christianity. This exposure, to echo Behar, is not to be vulnerable simply to vent, but rather to employ a cathartic and evocative *why* in my writing. If the church has broken my heart repeatedly, why do I stay?

My broken heart

Imagine you're sitting on an airplane—the enclosed spaces of air travel always make for interesting observations of strangers—and you notice that the young woman on your left, watching the in-flight entertainment, is crying. You can see that it's a romantic comedy, so you imagine that she's just lost love and that the story, instead of making her laugh, is evoking tears—perhaps tears for a girlfriend who left her. Then you notice that the young woman wearing a clerical collar on the other side of you is reading a book. And she too is crying. But why?

I was that young woman. The one with the clerical collar weeping into her book of theology. I wrote the preceding paragraph on United Airlines flight 975 from Geneva, Switzerland to Washington, DC in 2006. I had recently been launched, unsuspecting, into leadership in the ecumenical movement. I sat on that airplane reading a book and trying to hold back tears. The clerical collar is a touch of poetic licence. Despite wanting to visibly mark myself then as a priest in a still very male-dominated profession (to the horror of many non-collar wearing colleagues in the United Church of Canada at the time, although in the intervening years collar-wearing has come back into style), I very rarely make my religious "other-ness" quite that obvious in public.

So why was I crying? I was crying for the same reason as my fictional lesbian protagonist who'd just lost her partner; I have a broken heart. The church and society have both broken my heart repeatedly. In her controversial scholarship (controversial in that her Cherokee ancestry is questioned, not in relation to the brilliance of her thought), Andrea Smith makes powerful comparisons between the religious conquest of Indigenous Peoples and the sexual conquest of Native women.[11] Despite being battered theologically on a semi-constant (yet infuriatingly unpredictable) basis, I am staying with the church. I am staying with the ecumenical movement. I am staying with my covertly and overtly racist siblings in Christ whom I believe also endeavour to become Christians one day.

My experience of the triune God has been incredibly profound—palpable almost. I truly believe that I am called to share that experience—the good news—with the world. Sometimes the people of the church make me want to throw my hands up in utter defeat and walk away. And then I see injustice in the world, and I know—*I know*—that our faith has a liberating word that speaks justice and truth to power, and I am liberated myself; I am renewed; I am made strong through the liberating love of the Christ and the passion of the Holy Spirit, and I am back. It is in those in-between epiphanic moments when I am in the depths of institutional despair that my heart is broken over, and over again. And yet I stay. I keep going back to my abusive life-partner. I love the church. I can't leave.

So why do I stay? Because just as there are fallible children of God who intentionally or unintentionally hurt me and each other in the church, just as there are people who cannot see how they create and perpetuate systems of injustice in churches that are supposed to be—who are *called to be*—fighting injustice, there are others who see the world as I do. It is not *exactly* like an emotionally or physically abusive relationship; I think my staying is important for the sake of the church, whereas I would never encourage a survivor of abuse to stay with their abuser. There are those who inspire me, people who have left tracks in the snow for me in the depths of winter. There are many in my generation in North America who have abandoned the institutionalized church. I watch in awe as they harness the positive energy of the internet and social media to congregate and protest a globalizing economy that is increasing the gap between rich and poor at an exponential rate. I see them with placards in city squares and at national monuments insisting that their activist voices be heard. And I know I am no different. The power structures of the church need to be radically altered.

I am ambivalent about the efficacy of the ways we have been trying to do this in churches. On the one hand, I hear from colleagues that in many cases the dollars coming into mainline Protestant churches are declining rapidly. When change is suggested, especially when that change requires investment in those individuals and communities who have been made marginal, and the question is raised, "Who will pay for this change?" I find myself muttering under my breath, "You're just tired of paying for colonialism." The unspoken response I hear back quite clearly is "We *are* tired of paying for it." It seems as if the dominant institutions in North America have come to believe they are no longer colonialist in their thoughts or actions. In my mind, sixty years of partial financial atonement does not make up for more than five hundred years of destruction of multiple social orders and the continued dehumanization and patronization of Indigenous Peoples. But my opinion will not bring blood from a stone.

This reminds me of the dynamics that occur when men are disempowered by economic collapse and are no longer able to fulfil their culturally gender-conditioned roles as "providers." If the man was part of the dominant culture, he will often become either grandiose in his thinking or develop an inferiority complex. He will lash out, either up at the system or down at those below him. On the other hand, if he is part of a community made marginal and there is no one below him at whom to lash out, he will engage in lateral wounding by hurting his family, his friends, and others trapped in the same system of despair and oppression. Cornel West identified this tendency in young African American men in his book *Race Matters*,[12] but I also see it in other communities of those made marginal.

So, the patriarchal church is mourning its demasculinization. Embodying the classic "victim-offender" dynamic I described above, I hear men (yes, it is usually men) saying there is no money left to continue to *carry* the poor and the oppressed, forgetting that they and their forebears *created* the poor and oppressed. They argue that the poor and oppressed have been actively lifted up since World War II, implying that if these others would simply assimilate, they would succeed. Of course, this notion of success is defined according to colonialist thinking. The discourse has become: "The Global South is bankrupting the Global North." Yet this cannot be true on the church level unless it is true on the global economic level. No, it is the other way around: the Global North continues to bankrupt the Global South by razing its peoples and places for market profit.

In my view, the problem is that for the first time in history, the churches in the Global North no longer have the money, but they still have the power. The paternalistic atonement through massive block grants or comprehensive settlements and "aid" to the marginalized over the past sixty years or so has created unhealthy dependencies that are no longer sustainable. I say dependency because although the language states that the church is becoming "inclusive," that inclusivity comes with a caveat: do not challenge the status quo. Theologians who confront the power dynamics in the global ecumenical movement are either ostracized or forced to conform. The church has tried to buy its freedom from the guilt of its past without coming to the realization that the past is in no way behind us. We are still wearing its oppressive structures like a smothering garment. So now that there is no longer the money to attempt to buy freedom through development and aid, the truth is unmasked: the North still has the power. This truth is further exposed by the demographic shift in global Christianity: the Global South has the people, but the people do not have the power.

My work echoes that of Māori and Tongan theologians Jenny Te Paa and Jione Havea who ask, "Whose interests do contextual theologies serve?"[13] In my view, despite the church's efforts to honour the contextual differences between Global South and Global North, despite the billions of dollars it has given to the South since the end of World War II, the church continues to serve the North. I believe there are three reasons for this. One, the North has not given of what it has freely: its gifts have always been conditional. Two, dominant societies see any dialogue as "a means to a solution" rather than an end in itself. In other words, they are always trying to "fix the situation" for the oppressed. And three, the North still functions according to a global economy that is based on the principle of competition for scarce resources.

These three ideas are at the root of what breaks my heart. They are the baseline from where I start to propose how missiology might be transformed for the twenty-first century. But first I must defend why an Indigenous theology, and specifically an Indigenous theology of mission, must be, by definition, a political theology. The primary reason for this, in my opinion, is that to resolve the political issues that face the relationship between Indigenous and non-Indigenous communities there must be dialogue. But Indigenous perspectives, as I have learned from my friends to the south of this continent, uphold the liberationist perspective that dialogue is not just a means to the solution. Dialogue, itself, is the objective. When dialogue is seen as simply a means toward solving problems facing Indigenous communities, that is a binary epistemological problem that posits "us" vs. "them." An inclusive, pedagogical perspective that harnesses the best of what we know, have reclaimed, or have created in the current Indigenous context, sees that for both the oppressed and oppressors to be liberated, the dialogue itself is the key to undoing the knot of this colonialist challenge to our continued existence.

A Note on Style

WHEN I WAS pursuing doctoral studies, there wasn't really any consensus about styles relating to how to write from an Indigenous perspective or relating to the social constructs of race. At the time, George "Tink" Tinker had flipped some historical conventions of writing on their head to decentre "euroChristian" cultural normativity. He did not capitalize race categories; he used indigenous, white, black, etc. And some terms like european, western, and christian were spelled with a lowercase as an act of protest.

Since then, there has been, especially in the Canadian context, much more advancement on how Indigenous Peoples should be treated in written form, and how Indigenous Voices should be represented and respected on the page.

In *American Indian Liberation: A Theology of Sovereignty*, Tink Tinker, like many other Indigenous scholars in the US and Canada, identifies non-Indigenous communities as "Settler societies" and then refers to the Indigenous Peoples of the northern half of this continent as American Indian or by tribal names.

In *Kanata*, what is known as the nation state Canada, we use additional terms: First Nations, Métis, Inuit, Native, and sometimes (although less and less so) Aboriginal. We also use Status or Non-Status Indian to identify whether one is legally considered "Indian" by the Government of Canada under *The Indian Act* and is thereby registered with a particular tribal authority. In general, I refer to Indigenous Peoples as "Indigenous" and, wherever possible, by distinct tribal names. Occasionally I use other terms out of habit, to make a point, or when directly quoting others.

I capitalize White as a signifier of White privilege. To refer to communities who settled in North America more than one or two generations ago, I use Settler. I sometimes use the term Arrivant, as Chickasaw scholar Jodi Byrd does, to represent subsequent waves of immigration not represented by Settlers and their progeny. Byrd was inspired by Afro-Caribbean poet Kamau Brathwaite's use of Arrivants "to signify those people forced into the Americas through the violence of European and Anglo-American colonialism and imperialism around the globe." I sometimes do the same although, since Arrivant is not commonly used, I often simply distinguish by saying Indigenous and non-Indigenous. I use "dominant society" to refer to Settler and Arrivant communities together. Where I do use Settler and Arrivant I capitalize, because they are constructs. Although Tinker does not capitalize Indigenous, in Canada this has become common practice and so I do capitalize Indigenous throughout. I have engaged extensively with Latin American writers, and while Latinx has been used often in North America to provide a gender-neutral term to the traditionally gendered Latino/Latina, "x" is not a sound that is used in Spanish, so where appropriate I have adopted the Spanish gender-inclusive term Latine.

The use of Indigenist

By Indigenist[14] I mean collective Indigenous perspectives (so, a simpler term for pan-Indigenous) and sometimes those perspectives of allies to Indigenous thought. For example, Andrea Smith's Cherokee heritage has been repeatedly called into question, but the spirit and content of her work superbly expresses Indigenous concerns, and her work is still considered by some, therefore, as Indigenist, if it cannot be securely claimed as Indigenous.

Elements of Indigenous Style

Gregory Younging's *Elements of Indigenous Style: A Guide for Writing By and About Indigenous Peoples* now guides my work. Where his work is silent, I use *The Associated Press Stylebook,* 57th Edition. I differ from *The AP Stylebook* when referencing racial constructs, where I've adopted the practice of the National Institutes of Health in the United States, capitalizing

> all references to race, including White. This is a divergence from AP style. Writing white in the lowercase could give the impression that it is the default, neutral, or a standard. The capital letter for a racial identity is not intended to elevate, but to situate.[15]

I italicize words that are Indigenous in origin, except when (wherever possible and known by me) the word has been subsumed by the English language. I am just learning how many words in a Canadian context are Indigenous in origin, so any oversight is unintentional. Where an Indigenous word has been absorbed into English and I am aware of the original word in the Indigenous language, I italicize and use the original word: *Tkaronto* for Toronto, *Kanata* for Canada. Here is a short list of terms that should be capitalized, according to *Elements of Indigenous Style*:

Aboriginal
First Nations
First Peoples
Indigenous
Inuit/Inuk
Métis
Survivor
Chief
Clan; Clan System; Matriarch
Creator; Creation
Elder
Indigenous Voice
Longhouse
Big House
Medicine Man; Medicine Woman
Midewiwin/Midewin
Oral Tradition
Potlatch

Protocols (cultural)
Sacred Pipe Ceremony; Pipe Carrier
Seven Fires
Sundance
Sweat Lodge
Traditional Knowledge
Vision Quest
Warrior Society
Wampum; Wampum Belt
Indigenous Land; Indigenous Title; Traditional Territory
Indigenous Right
Status Indian
Treaty Right

I do not necessarily use all these terms in this book, but I follow Younging's rationale for terms representing Indigenous identities, Indigenous institutions, and Indigenous collective rights, and will assert the same logic in my treatment of those words in English.

Introduction

IN 1986, THE United Church of Canada offered a brief general apology to Indigenous Peoples in *Kanata*[16] for a history of colonialism and a theology of Christian mission that included the imposition of Euro-Western civilization as a prerequisite for Christian faith.[17] Over the past nearly four decades, dialogue has been deepening between the church and Indigenous Peoples on issues of faith, culture, colonialism, residential and boarding institutions (the so-called "schools"), racism, and oppression. In 2008, the Prime Minister of Canada with the support of the Canadian Assembly of First Nations announced and then launched a Truth and Reconciliation Commission to investigate and report on the history of Canadian residential schools, and to make recommendations for reconciliation. Reconciliation has become a key topic of conversation in communities of faith; both Indigenous and non-Indigenous people grapple with what it means to reconcile the traumatic histories of our shared colonial history. While the discourse in the United States has not until recently explicitly focused on residential schools or reconciliation (President Joe Biden made a historic first apology in Arizona in October 2024), the conversation can sometimes run parallel in important ways; although legal statuses of Indigenous Peoples in the two countries are very different, the lived realities of Indigenous communities in North America are very similar.

Reconciliation can be defined in many ways: to agree to an amicable truce; to become resigned to something that is not desired; to make compatible or consistent; and, theologically speaking, to be absolved of sin through confession and making penance. For me, none of these definitions fit. While the reconciliation of our cultures may be a goal in the future, I believe that without a deeper discussion of some of the underlying issues and the dynamics of continued colonialism, there is a danger that the dominant society will continue to direct the conversation based on the needs of the dominant at the expense of the needs of Indigenous communities.

The *Haíłzaqv*[18] Tribal Council has worked through community consultation over a period of years to develop its own understanding of reconciliation. In our language, *haíłzaqvla*, we use the word *haíłcístut* which means "to turn things around and make them right again."[19] This is more like the theological concept of repentance than reconciliation, and it is the model I prefer.

There are two foundational concepts that have shaped my approach to this work. First, I believe that theology matters: what we do/think/say about God, the spirit, and God incarnate *matters*. Our most profoundly held faith beliefs shape our thoughts and actions in ways that have real and tangible environmental and socio-political implications for the earth and the communities in which we live. Theology, as a discipline, holds value for the deepening of our faith, and the strengthening of our ethical responsibility to the earth and its communities. Theology requires us to think deeply and critically about life, the cosmos, and the land. It can also be poetic language that marries our actions and our faith.

The second concept is articulated by George "Tink" Tinker, who argues that all Indigenous theology is political theology.[20] Specifically, he says that "any useful commentary by American Indians speaking to the Indian context today must reflect on the political state of Indian affairs and the political hopes and visions for recovering the health and well-being of Indian communities."[21] I don't mean to draw necessarily on the formal Western tradition of "political theology" as begun by Johann Baptist Metz and continued by Jürgen Moltmann, Dorothee Söelle, and others (that is outside the scope of this current study), but rather to say that the political—i.e. laws, policies, and rights—must be considered as part of any theology that speaks to the Indigenous context.

Here is the point of this book: I do not believe that all narratives, all interpretations, all readings, and all contexts are "equal." This is the crux of what Gustavo Gutiérrez argued in *A Theology of Liberation: History, Politics and Salvation*. By saying that God has a "preferential option for the poor," Gutiérrez does not mean that God *favours* the poor (read: oppressed, and therefore Indigenous) over and above others.[22] He explains: "In some ways, *option* is perhaps the weakest word in the sentence. In English, the word merely connotes a choice between two things. In Spanish, however, it evokes the sense of commitment. The option for the poor is not optional but is incumbent upon every Christian."[23]

Liberationist thought calls on Christianity to commit to addressing the systems of injustice that cause oppression and the marginalization of entire communities. It does not call us to choose life only for the poor (as some fear when they ask, "Does God not love the rich?"), but rather to acknowledge that when systems of injustice persist, neither the marginalized nor the dominant are free. In this way, I hope to move towards a liberationist hope of freedom and open missiology by employing Indigenous epistemologies, by privileging Indigenist philosophy and theology alongside hegemonic Western thought patterns that have historically either eradicated or subjugated Indigenous Voices.

I will explore the ways Indigenous epistemologies become effective tools for a constructive theological enterprise because they do not employ the traditional binary dualisms and arguments on belief and justification of truth that have preoccupied Western epistemologies since Descartes. While traditional Indigenous epistemologies use different (and usually non-academic) language(s), in this book I use the language of the academy. This was required for my doctoral dissertation, which formed the basis of this book, but it is also intentional on my part because I find comfort and community in the academy as an Indigenous scholar.

In general, Indigenous epistemologies recognize multiple interpretations of truth and reality, and they do so from a pragmatically pedagogical grounding. As I will explain, the intent of such a position is not phenomenological but pedagogical. While there are multiple approaches to Western epistemologies

(Aristotle over Plato, to name an example), Western philosophies of knowledge have primarily been attempts to theorize what defines knowledge. I don't mean to say there has been no progress or diversity of opinion in post-Enlightenment Western philosophy, but, in general, definitions of knowledge remain phenomenological and based on formal logic as a sub-discipline of philosophy.

In contrast, Indigenist perspectives take what is known and extrapolate meaning from that truth rather than theorizing what defines truth and then measuring experience against that definition. To generalize, Western perspectives tend to be more deductive, and Indigenist perspectives tend to be more inductive. If we are to seek liberation, we must privilege Indigenist interpretations, lift up the narratives of the oppressed, and address and correct the narratives of the oppressors.

I will also examine Indigenous theologies concerned with mission, and theologies of mission that affect Indigenous realities. Indigenous epistemologies necessarily must shape missiology if we are to take into consideration the political concerns of the people. In this area, I draw on several important but disparate works that have influenced my critical theological work. I use the work of John Caputo and his Derridean approaches to deconstruction to explain the components of twentieth century missiology.

The synthesis of Indigenous epistemologies and Christian mission forms an intersectional constructive theology of Christian mission. Influenced by the work of process/constructive theologian Catherine Keller, this work is an open-ended theology that represents the liberative demands of Indigenist perspectives. In her 2008 *On the Mystery*, introducing constructive and process theology, Keller writes:

> Those who know suffering come closer to a truth about the creation: the future is open, alarmingly or promisingly. The way is not laid out in advance. Creation itself is in process. Our own way forward has not been charted. There may be no trail before us at all. Sometimes one can only move forward in faith: that is, in courage and confidence, not in a delusional certainty.[24]

My goal will be to examine what Christian mission looks like "from below" when written from a contemporary Indigenous perspective.

Keller argues that definitions of truth matter.[25] Much like the Indigenist perspectives I will present in chapter two, she acknowledges that there are multiple truths if one considers the touch of truth on experience. She argues:

> I am suggesting that [theology's] *truth* [the truth of the proposition "Jesus suffered because he loved us"] depends on the context of the spirit: is it in touch with the very *love* it names? Abstracted from its living relationships, even a proposition about divine love can be cited "in bad faith." It can be turned into a terrorizing absolute. Such abstraction from text and context, whereby a proposition can then be reinserted unilaterally into any life situation, is the temptation of all forms of truth-language, but above all of theology. It is the fertilizer of every atheism.[26]

Her point is one that weighs on me in this project. My words are not meant to criticize, but to critique with an integrity grounded in Indigenous realities. The desire to critique comes from a profound respect and love for Western theology, and, in fact, a sense of security and safety within the Western tradition that allows me to critique. While I hope that my words and arguments make an impact and that I can present a theological perspective that starts to reframe our understanding of mission and the church, I do so in a way that is motivated by the relational perspective articulated by Keller. My work always attempts to be in touch with the love it names.

Ultimately, I could choose to pursue the path of atheism in response to my personal perspective on the shortcomings of churches in relation to the struggles of Indigenous Peoples. If not atheism, then at least a rejection of the Christian faith in favour of a return to Indigenous spiritual practices. At times, those options have seemed attractive, and they are paths that some Indigenous people have chosen. And yet, alongside many other Indigenous people, I believe that there are truths in Christian faith that can promote justice and reconciliation if handled gently and used to foster relational connection. My personal journey as a Christian has been an attempt to show the world that there can be new paths for us to walk together as Indigenous and non-Indigenous Peoples. These paths are not the only ways, but simply possibilities that can lead us to a deeper understanding of Indigenous struggles and ways in which the whole church can respond to those struggles. Australian theologian Chris Budden identifies two dangers in the theological endeavour:

> [that the] context and experience [of people] are not taken seriously, and that they are not allowed or able to question, challenge, engage with the past in ways that bring them genuine life and wholeness (a complaint sometimes lodged by feminists and black people, for example). The second danger is that people only know a narrow part of the landscape. This narrowness occurs because each tradition has its own map (and thinks that this is the only map), and each local community has its own slightly amended version of the tradition's map.[27]

These dangers are, in part, why I remain a committed interdisciplinarian, and why this book is explicitly interdisciplinary in nature. By reading across disciplines and engaging in thoughtful dialogue with contributors to intercultural thought and Indigenous philosophy, I am attempting to broaden the horizons of both my own faith community and others shaped by traditional hegemonic Western worldviews. Interdisciplinary scholar Julie Thompson Klein reminds us that geopolitics influence the practice of interdisciplinary scholarship:

> Geopolitics are central to the conception of interdisciplinarity because, as Robert L. Scott put it, there is a "distinctly political face to the circumstances in which interdisciplinary efforts must thrive or not." Disciplinary structure is so deeply embedded in academic institutions that it is unusual to find an argument for interdisciplinarity that does not acknowledge that sociopolitical reality.[28]

Thompson Klein likens the practice of interdisciplinary study to entering a no man's land in the spaces between disciplines, and I use that image in this book.

I make use of the "interstitial model" of interdisciplinary studies, which Judith Berling describes as recognizing "the boundaries of disciplines but work[ing] between them . . . marked not by an adherence to disciplinary methodologies but by exploration of the 'negative,' 'unexplored' space between these methodologies. It recognizes boundaries of disciplines but does not work within them. It transgresses, synthesizes, etc."[29] I work in the spaces between my two fields of research: Indigenous epistemologies and theologies of mission. Traditionally in educational and curricula studies there are boundaries separating Indigenous epistemologies and missiology. Working between these two fields, I articulate a theology of mission from an Indigenous perspective. I believe the liminal space opened by this form of interdisciplinarity makes room for the expression of a deep longing to change the status quo.

Many Indigenous writers are angry at colonization and are working to reclaim our culture and identity. It is frustrating when, in the process of reclaiming our culture and identity, we are questioned about the authenticity of our "Indian-ness" or the degree to which we've assimilated. These questions are often posed most vociferously by Indigenous colleagues. I believe that fiction and poetry can help us connect history with our present reality and should be included in the academy as available alternatives to more traditional scholarly forms such as dissertations that are confined by the epistemological hegemonies I identify in this book. Because fiction and poetry are not as bound by scientific methods as research papers, for instance, they can express more powerfully how my heart is broken, and how the status quo needs changing.

This is why I use constructive theology as a methodology in this book. I have found the practice of constructive theological scholarship (as opposed to "systematic" theology)[30] to be the most liberating form of theological scholarship. Following from Keller's desire to grasp a future that is "open, alarmingly and promisingly . . . [moving forward] not in a delusional certainty," my intensely personal commitment to addressing Indigenous suffering frees me to write out of faith rather than anger at the sometimes-delusional certainty of traditional systematic theology.

In this book I describe the political nature of Indigenous theology through an analysis of the current strengths and weaknesses of the theological concept *missio Dei*. *Missio Dei* originated as a concept before Augustinian times. It appears in the writings of Gregory of Nyssa, Ignatius, and others, and translates from Latin as "God's mission." *Missio Dei* became popular during the mid-twentieth century mission consultations of the World Council of Churches (WCC) and International Missionary Council (IMC) as distinct from *missiones ecclesiolae*—meaning "the mission of the churches." Church leaders distinguished between the two to shift the focus from churches doing mission, to mission-centred churches. That attempt to extricate mission from colonialism failed. Re-envisioning missions as something that belonged to God rather than the church did not put a stop to colonialism or oppression; it merely obscured who should be held accountable for oppression enacted in the name of church missions. Perhaps the more tragic and dangerous outcome of the elevation of *missio Dei* as a concept is that the term never became fully articulated or defined. The distinction between *missio Dei* and the mission of the church remains, in my mind, both subtle and important. Although *missio Dei* has rightfully come under critique in the last decades (see chapters three and four), I believe that Christian faith as expressed through churches *should* remain mission-centred.

Growing up *Haíłzaqv* in *Kanata* I came to associate mission and evangelism with colonialism and Western cultural hegemony. This is not only due to the historic roles played by mainline Protestant churches in the conquest of North America, but also to the continuing practices of mainline and, increasingly, evangelical missionaries to the Pacific Northwest Coast. Our isolated communities are still inundated with missionaries who continue to perpetuate abusive models of missionary theology and praxis that insist on the wholesale rejection of traditional *Hąíłzaqv* (and other Indigenous) culture(s) and emphasize personal conversion and the acceptance of Jesus Christ as one's personal Lord and saviour. Earlier in my theological education I had a revelatory moment when I celebrated my own intellectual re-claiming of "evangelism" once I came to understand the meaning of *εὐαγγέλιον (euangélion)*, as "the good news" in biblical Greek. I want to reclaim my voice as an evangelist—for there certainly is good news to be found in our Christian story.

This book has three parts, each represented in the title. "Wearing a broken Indigene heart" is an exploration of the political realities that continue to shape Indigenous thinking. While the term "Indigene" may be unfamiliar,

I use it to emphasize the personal and subjective quality of my Indigenous identity. "On the sleeve of Christian Mission" is meant to make transparent the strengths and shortcomings of this missiological concept. No longer in the title, my doctoral dissertation also included "Bearing Witness," which represented the constructive act of both political truth-telling and embracing what is ever hopeful in Christian theology and mission despite what breaks my heart. While one could argue that because we have hearts, we bear Christian witness in love through Christ, I use the metaphor of "wearing my heart on my sleeve" because of the emotional forthrightness I bring to both Indigenous political issues and my faith.

In this introduction I want to outline the three sections that form the basis for my arguments in subsequent chapters. First, I highlight some of the missiology of South African theologian David Bosch. For over three decades, his major work *Transforming Mission: Paradigm Shifts in Theology of Mission* was a starting point for mainline Protestant missiology in North America.[31] While his work is dated, I will bring forward a key few of his concepts and leave the rest in the past. As I'll explain later, Bosch suggested thirteen separate ways for us to think about mission. Four of his suggestions, I believe, are ripe for deeper theological engagement in the twenty-first century.

In the second part of this introduction, I summarize George "Tink" Tinker's scholarship on Christian mission. Both his more hopeful *American Indian Liberation* and his older *Missionary Conquest: The Gospel and Native American Cultural Genocide*[32] provide important insights into the specific historical relationship between Indigenous communities in North America and Christian mission. In *Missionary Conquest*, Tinker argues that missionaries, both historically and presently, participate in genocide. Naming the genocidal tendency of Christian mission is not meant as a punishment or a condemnation of those who unwittingly participate, but rather "out of a sense that this is part of [north] America's unfinished business."[33] I argue that much of the "unfinished business" identified by Tinker in 1993 and beyond is still unfinished in 2024. Discourse relating to reconciliation remains fruitless without deep analysis of colonialism, how missiology served as a cover for colonialism, and how colonialism is still occurring in North American society in the twenty-first century.

In the third section of this introduction, I examine concepts of postcolonialism, post-colonialism, anti-colonialism, decolonialism, and why they are distinct. The distinctions are important from an Indigenous point of view because, although the differences may be subtle, they get to the heart of the unique experience of *fait accompli* colonialism (that is to say, when European colonialism is no longer a context that can be reversed—it becomes the new normal). There may be places where locating Indigenous voices within a broader postcolonial discourse is helpful (as I argued in the preface), while there may also be places where it may be more appropriate and impactful to set them apart as distinctly decolonial or anti-colonial.

Revisiting *Transforming Mission*

South African missiologist David J. Bosch's magnum opus *Transforming Mission: Paradigm Shifts in Theology of Mission* was probably one of the most consistently assigned texts in mission studies in North American mainline Protestant theological education at the end of the twentieth century. While his missiology is limited in some very significant places (he has little to contribute to theology of religions, religious pluralism, globalization, or issues of race, sexuality, or gender) and is now dated, if he is read alongside a diversity of other thinkers, those gaps can become clear and force the reader to interrogate his arguments in fruitful ways.[34] I argue in the chapter on Indigenous and Western epistemologies that choosing Indigenous epistemologies over Western epistemologies is a false dichotomy; the point of Indigenous epistemological difference is that it is inclusive of multiple truths. It is possible to embrace Western perspectives as valuable while also honouring Indigenous wisdom and experience. This is how I use Bosch; critiques notwithstanding, there is value and wisdom in specific parts of his work. *Transforming Mission* begins with a summary of mission in different historical epochs and an observation that mission in the late twentieth century was poised for a major paradigm shift. Bosch recognized that postmodernism and postcolonialism would both influence missiology in the twenty-first century, but he died in 1992 and therefore did not get to see his proposed "ecumenical paradigm" incorporated into missiology in this century.

I first became excited about missiology as a field of study when I read excerpts from *Transforming Mission*. This text was the reason I decided to pursue doctoral studies in this area. In consultations held by the World Council of Churches, Bosch emphasized the importance of Christian unity and encouraged engagement with global perspectives on Christianity. Bosch echoed another prominent Protestant missiologist of the twentieth century, Lesslie Newbigin. Both received theological training in the Global North but were influenced profoundly by their lived experience of Christianity in the Global South. In fact, Bosch played a significant role in shaping South African theological thought during the later Apartheid era. Although he came under sharp criticism for it, Bosch chose to stay and fight his contemporaries in the denomination of his ordination, the Dutch Reformed Church, rather than leaving for a denomination that vocally opposed the Apartheid system. His struggle against Apartheid was not named in his work—his contemporaries felt he should have been theologically explicit and public in his criticism. Sadly, he did not come to this position before his untimely death in 1992.

Rather than taking a particular text and using it as *the* biblical basis for mission, as many past and present theologians have, Bosch offered an overall study of the New Testament as a document of mission. He presented the gospels of Matthew and Luke as well as the books of Acts and the epistles as holistic biblical paradigms for mission. The Great Commission text found in Matthew 28.16-20 is often presented as a call to the church to engage in mission. Many writers, such as Christopher Duraisingh and Jayakiran Sebastian, offer alternative scriptural bases for missiology by pointing to the book of Acts. Bosch also resisted the temptations of foundationalism[35] by refusing to offer only one passage.

Bosch's approach was not without problems. He omitted the gospels of Mark and John, for instance. He also dismissed the Hebrew Scriptures as not missionary in nature. If his intention was to avoid the imposition of a uniquely Christian theology (i.e. missiology) onto texts that were Jewish in origin, that does not mean that the Hebrew texts do not offer important potential support for missiological studies and practice in a Christian context. At the very least, Christian theology should examine the relationship between the Christian texts and the Hebrew Scriptures as they relate to mission, if only so as not to engage unintentionally in anti-Semitism or supersessionism.

The final section of *Transforming Mission* identified the emergence of a postmodern historical paradigm together with an emerging ecumenical missionary paradigm. Bosch outlined the ways in which Enlightenment thinking has been challenged by postmodernity. Bosch identified six signs that he believed signaled the end of the modern era: 1) the expansion of rationality, 2) a decreased certainty in "objectivity," 3) the rediscovery of the teleological, 4) the emergence of challenges to "progress" thinking, 5) the creation of a fiduciary framework, and 6) the elevation of interdependence above independence and individualism.[36] I find these to be insightful categorizations of the shift from modern to postmodern, though the shift has not been as complete or as clean as Bosch made it out to be. I tend to think of the arrival of postmodernity more as the peeling of layers from an onion rather than a shift in paradigm. I also feel that modernist thinking still holds value to some parts of life in a globalizing world. The more abusive and oppressive aspects of modernity, such as the Global North's unwavering support for end-stage capitalist economics, are particularly tenacious, and postmodern challenges to such firmly entrenched ideas can only peel them away layer by layer.

Section 12 of *Transforming Mission* offers significant discussion of thirteen different elements of Bosch's emerging ecumenical missionary paradigm, some of which are still useful today. The thirteen elements are: 1) mission as the church with others, 2) mission as *missio Dei*, 3) mission as mediating salvation, 4) mission as the quest for justice, 5) mission as evangelism, 6) mission as contextualization, 7) mission as liberation, 8) mission as inculturation, 9) mission as common witness, 10) mission as ministry by the whole people of God, 11) mission as witness to people of other living faiths, 12) mission as theology, and 13) mission as action in hope. Each of these elements offers insight for mission in the twenty-first century. I will therefore provide some general comments on his emerging paradigm as well as highlight a few of the thirteen elements I feel to be still important.

It is important to note what was *not* included in Bosch's *Transforming Mission*. Given that Bosch lived and worked under extreme duress in Apartheid South Africa, it is at once both understandable and surprising that issues of racism are nowhere explicitly articulated. Even though he highlighted contextual theology as a feature of emerging ecumenical missiology, he did not engage in contextual theology himself. While he was a White South African opposed to Apartheid, he never once mentioned Apartheid as the context from which he was writing. Two subsequent volumes, edited by Willem Saayman and Klippies Kritzinger, *Mission in Bold Humility: David Bosch's Work Considered*[37] and *Mission in Creative Tension: A Dialogue with David Bosch*,[38] offer a variety of critiques of and engagements with *Transforming Mission*. Many of the articles in these two volumes argue that by staying silent on African issues in general, and Black theology and Apartheid in particular, Bosch did not do justice to theology in Africa.

It is acknowledged that Bosch took the position that he should not choose sides in his writing, but critics such as Kritzinger argue there is a missiological imperative to choose. Kritzinger positions himself as an ally of Black theology in Apartheid South Africa and belongs to a movement that went further than Bosch in condemning injustice. Bosch's silence is echoed in the American academy's silence on justice issues today, clearly revealing unfinished theological work for me and my Indigenous colleagues.

Bosch also failed in his writing to confront sexism and misogyny in theology, mission, and the church. While he occasionally raised the question of women's ordination, he only did so in the context of the challenge of ecumenical differences in ecclesiological self-understanding, rather than as a matter of gender justice. This is surprising given that his work was developing alongside ecumenical theological studies of sexism and the creation of Just Communities of Women and Men in the church, most notably as demonstrated in Constance Parvey's *The Community of Women and Men in the Church*,[39] commonly known as the "Sheffield Report" in ecumenical circles.

Other conspicuous silences in *Transforming Mission* include the absence of any treatment of creation and environmental concerns or discourse on economic justice and the growing gap between rich and poor in both local and global economies. These issues can hardly be separated from colonialism and poverty in the past or the present. While awareness of many of today's most urgent environmental crises postdate Bosch, there were many global environmental issues of which he would have been aware: acid rain, rising sea levels, clear-cut logging, desertification, species at risk, pollution from mining, drought, and access to safe drinking water.

Lastly, Bosch seemed to limit his treatment of Roman Catholicism to the medieval period; I would argue that many of the elements of the ecumenical paradigm originated in and are driven by Roman Catholic missiology. I do not mean that concepts like contextualization, liberation, inculturation, and the whole people of God are not ecumenical, but that they took root in explicitly Roman Catholic contexts. "Mission as Common Witness" comes from the document of the Joint Working Group of the World Council of Churches with the Roman Catholic Church.[40]

Among Bosch's thirteen elements, I hold four to be most important in the context of the twenty-first century, and ripe for renewed and deeper theological engagement. First, "mission as church with others" remains important because it highlights the need for solidarity with the oppressed and those made marginal in society, including those colonized by missions. This idea also takes on new meaning in the contemporary context of twenty-first century wars waged by the US and its allies against countries which are Muslim majority with increasingly small Christian minorities. Not only are we called to accompany all peoples living under systems of oppression, but we must also find prophetic ways to support and walk with Christian minorities (or, indeed, any religious minorities) who are living in situations of civil or global military conflict. This would include not only Afghanistan and Iraq, but also other Middle Eastern and North African countries such as Iran, Syria, Lebanon, Israel and the Occupied Palestinian Territories, Yemen, and Egypt as well as Asian countries including Myanmar, Indonesia, Sri Lanka, Pakistan, India, and North Korea.

Secondly, I highlight "mission as the quest for justice." This position is supported by the Indigenous theologians of Latin America who are strongly influenced by classical liberation theologians and indeed move even further towards freedom than they did. In my view, missiology has too often focused on the salvation of individuals and the propagation of the church and has considered the quest for justice a lesser priority. By contrast, among Indigenous communities in Central America, biblical and theological studies are deeply engaged with the struggles of the people against foreign and domestic governments and companies causing great environmental and social harm. Many ecumenical statements identify the sin of oppression that manifests itself in the geopolitical socio-economic status quo of our increasingly globalized world. The quest for justice is inseparable from mission.

While I hold that the third concept, "mission as liberation," is important, I think it is crucial to take it even further than some liberation theologians in Latin America do. I believe mission as liberation should be the basis for our analyses of missiology, economics, and race. Liberation theology has traditionally used economics to interrogate theology, however very few theological scholars have examined the racialization of poverty. Bosch addresses development theory in his section on liberation, but not its sister, dependency theory, nor its influence on liberation theology. Liberation theologies have also not adequately addressed justice issues for minorities in North America, although that is slowly changing. At the advent of liberation theology in Latin America, the marginalized poor were the majority of the population. This allowed them to build momentum for their cause in ways that minority populations such as the Dalit in India or Indigenous groups in North America could not. Understanding this context is essential to the study of mission. Further, liberation theology will always fail when its focus is only on liberation of the oppressed and not accompanied by conscientization, or critical consciousness, that results in liberation of the oppressors.

Last, and perhaps most important among Bosch's ecumenical missional concepts, is "mission as theology." In my experience, both the ecumenical movement and the study of missiology have become somewhat inbred. I don't mean to say that these sub-disciplines of theology are fully closed to outsiders or exclusivist, but that they continue to draw on the same traditions and on the same pools of thought, missing out on an ever-expanding and exciting body of scholarship that has grown out of postmodern and postcolonial challenges to modern theology. While feminisms in the twenty-first century continue to present ever-more nuanced and intersectional views of gender in theology, their insights remain conspicuously absent from missiology. Likewise, queer theory and queer theology—except for Cheri DiNovo's *Que(e)rying Evangelism: Growing the Church from the Outside In*[41]—have had relatively no impact on missiology. Neither has Dalit or Indigenous theology, at least not in the North American context.

In addition to the areas I identified where Bosch's influential work is incomplete regarding Indigenous theology, I depart from him in two places. I have written elsewhere about the importance of engaging in power analysis for missiology. Yet I do not think I have gone far enough in this respect. For analyses of mission, church, and theology to be complete, they must look not only at politics, economics, and sociology, but also at finance. I use the word "finance" rather than "economics" because I don't only mean our economic decisions, but also the very tangible access to wealth and credit: money. Jayakiran Sebastian also names this omission in his essay "Interrogating *missio Dei*: From the Mission of God towards Appreciating our Mission to God in India Today."[42] Money, in my experience, still comes with strings attached. I develop this idea further in chapter five by discussing Amartya Sen's economic theories that link different types of freedoms and *un*freedoms.

Despite the best efforts of churches in the Global North, *missio Dei* has not liberated the churches with the resources from paternalistic dynamics in their relationship with churches in the Global South. Interrogating the continued usefulness of the concept of *missio Dei* and explicit analysis and theological discourse on the issue of money and mission are two areas that need further development than what Bosch has offered in *Transforming Mission*.

Missionary Conquest: The Indigenous Experience

Indigenous revisions, both oral and academic, of traditional historiography are shedding light on the colonization of the Americas. Russell Means writes:

> All my life, I've had to listen to rhetoric about the United States being a model of freedom and democracy, the most uniquely enlightened and humanitarian country in history, a "nation of laws" which, unlike

> others, has never pursued policies of conquest and aggression . . . Well I've got a news flash for everybody here. It's a lie. The whole thing's a lie and it always has been.[43]

I could offer the same critique of *Kanata*'s view of itself as a model democracy that is polite, benevolent, and peacekeeping. To tell the true story of Indigenous genocide, dispossession, disruption, and dislocation is to challenge North American identity in such a radical way that the response of the dominant society is to shame, challenge, deny, ignore, and defend. Ward Churchill, the controversial former professor of ethnic studies at University of Colorado Boulder, writes, "The American holocaust was and remains unparalleled, both in terms of its magnitude and the degree to which its goals were met, and in terms of the extent to which its ferocity was sustained over time by not one but several participating groups."[44]

Tinker also insists that we look at the genocidal roots of the history of the Americas. Pre-contact populations of Indigenous Peoples in the Americas are estimated at 125 million or more. That would make this genocide the most historically vast in terms of numbers of bodies, but also in terms of culture. "Cultural genocide is more subtle than overt military genocide, yet it is no less devastating to a people," writes Tinker.[45] He defines cultural genocide as "the effective destruction of a people by systematically or systemically (intentionally or unintentionally to achieve other goals), destroying, eroding, or undermining the integrity of the culture and system of values that defines a people and gives them life."[46] He highlights the ways in which missionary activity in North America almost always attacked the very culture and system of values of Indigenous Peoples.

Indigenous writings on the physical and cultural genocide, overall, tend to be explicit, whereas non-Indigenous writing tends to ignore, to take genocide as a historical fact without acknowledging present political or cultural consequences, or to minimize its impact. For example, Stephen Neill's comprehensive *A History of Christian Missions* acknowledges colonial conquest, but avoids describing it as genocide:

> Again and again in our survey we have seen Christianity striving not to be a European religion. But on the whole its attempts were far from successful. Whether we like it or not, it is the historic fact that the great expansion of Christianity coincided in time with the world-wide and explosive expansion of Europe that followed on the Renaissance; that the colonizing powers were the Christian powers; that a whole variety of compromising relationships existed between missionaries and governments; and that in the main Christianity was carried forward on the wave of *Western* prestige and power.[47]

He later goes on to lament the changing idea of mission in post-colonial Africa: "A missionary was still needed, but only Africans, perhaps, could show Africans the faith in the African context. The idea of the European missionary, which lies at the heart of so much of this book, faded as the social and religious context changed."[48] The fact that the changing face of Christian mission is something for Neill to lament reinforces his earlier comment that attempts for Christian mission to be anything other than a European expression of Christianity have largely failed.

Tinker shows how the missionary movement's myopia to its inculturated Western values served both colonial governments and private interests in the colonization of the Americas:

> The culpability of the individual missionaries for imposing their culture on Native Americans and perpetuating the lie of white superiority was in actuality prescribed from the outset by European and Euroamerican social structures. That is to say, it was impossible for any missionary to avoid complicity in the genocide of Native American peoples.[49]

The idea of White superiority is acknowledged by scholars of missiology as a historic dynamic, but there remains a largely unchallenged assumption that this White superiority is a historical artifact rather than a contemporary social dynamic, informed by theology. From the civil rights movement until the mid-twenty teens, there has been a decrease in referential—or overt—racism; however, inferential racism—systemic and structured racialization of inequality—remained alive and well in North America.[50] Sadly, referential racism is once again on the rise.

Professor of Black Studies and Sociology George Lipsitz points out that "Whites may or may not be openly racists in their personal decisions or private interactions with others, but they nonetheless benefit systematically from the structural impediments to minority access to quality housing, schools, and jobs."[51] A justice-informed missiology cannot ignore this dynamic and, in fact, challenges us to expose and root out the systemic injustices.

The ways that Christian mission has benefited from or strengthened the structural impediments to Indigenous thriving in the Americas is the basis for any contemporary contextual missiology. Both referential and inferential racism are very much alive in the churches today, and it is of the utmost importance that racism be understood as not just impactful at the individual level but is seen through the wider lens of historic cultural and physical genocide.

Delineating Discussions on Post / Post- / De / Anti-Colonization

In the introduction to a 2004 article in *Mission Studies*, theologian Joerg Rieger quotes Bosch repeating a now infamous saying from 1913: "To missionize is to colonize, to colonize is to missionize."[52] Claiming that the colonial period is now generally conceived as over (an argument that needs re-evaluation in a North American context), Rieger writes, "Much of theology and mission has followed along, happily assuming the end of colonialism but wasting little thought about what it means to live in a postcolonial society."[53] This is, in part, what led to the mid-century concepts of *missio Dei* as distinct from *missiones ecclesiolae*.

Theologians of a more leftist persuasion, eager to distance themselves from a church practice so intimately connected with colonization, abandoned missiology altogether, and missiologists eager to explore what they perceived to be a liberated concept of mission have largely failed to keep up with the progression of theology as a discipline. This means that the liberative potential of missiology for theology and for the church has been stunted. Joerg Rieger names this issue:

> Few mainline theologians would defend the ventures of colonial Christianity. But have we truly overcome our colonial legacies? Do we even understand what the basic problems of colonial Christianity were? Is this case really closed? Can we return to business as usual? These questions impose themselves as soon as we leave the safe havens of "first world" mainline Christianity. Encounters with Christians from other parts of the world who bear many of the marks of both colonialism and neocolonialism in their own bodies, and even encounters with Christians at home subjected to internal colonialism and neocolonialism, might teach us that we must not move on too quickly.[54]

Rieger's questions are important. And yet, read from a North American Indigenous perspective, they raise a concern about the disappearance of Indigenous Peoples from all North American concerns—intellectual or otherwise. Why is it that we need to have encounters with Christians from other parts of the world to meet those who bear marks of colonialism and neocolonialism? I see them quite clearly here at home.

I know Joerg Rieger—and his commitment to decolonization, antiracism, and solidarity-building is solid. In fact, he has written explicitly about the impacts of colonization on Indigenous Peoples elsewhere. It remains a sensitivity for Indigenous Peoples in North America when our struggles are subsumed into a larger global decolonial context because of the erasure of so many of our histories here. And—as I will argue later—we also don't need to subscribe to binary dualisms—the colonized here face many of the same struggles and legacies of trauma as the colonized everywhere.

This is all to say that the discourse around colonization and colonialism is not simple. If colonization is understood as the political control over another's territory, occupation with Settlers, and economic exploitation, then there are some distinct terms in relation to that concept that need explanation at the outset of this book. I define the "colonial period" as the period between 1492 and the First World War, when the European superpowers were actively seeking to take political control over foreign lands, supported by the Roman Catholic church and later by Protestant churches.[55] I use "post-colonial" to refer to the period after active colonization. Most African and some Asian countries fall into what I would term the post-colonial period, having reached a state of independence, either through armed or peaceful resistance. I use "postcolonial" without a hyphen as Bill Ashcroft does—"to discuss the various cultural effects of colonization."[56]

In *Decolonization and the Decolonized*, Algerian theorist Albert Memmi examines the mindsets of the colonized in a post-colonial context. By critiquing the rampant poverty, corruption, and internalized oppression in the formerly colonized nation, and the assimilation of the immigrants who settle in the countries of the former colonizer, Memmi points to the failings of the postcolonial project.[57] While this work is certainly useful in critiquing the effects of decades of post-colonial life, especially in independent Latin American and African states, it speaks very little to the context of Indigenous life in North America.

The editors of *Postcolonial Theologies: Divinity and Empire* outline a helpful definition of the diverse ways in which postcolonial thought has developed into its own critical theory:

> First, one does not want to fall into a very common confusion: that "postcolonial theory" is presuming the end of colonialism. "Post" in this discourse never means simply "after" but also "beyond"—as an ethical intention and direction. *Western* imperialism is the frame of reference for the term "postcolonial," which emerges in the struggles of the colonies of Europe for their independence.[58]

The focus of this postcolonial theory, according to Keller, Nausner, and Rivera, is targeting the modern understanding of identity.[59] As theorists of postcolonial dynamics, Gayatri Spivak, Edward Said, and Homi Bhabha identify subjectivity and identity politics, the blurring of geopolitical and economic lines, and the impacts of colonization and post-colonialism on human bodies as particularly important.

For many Indigenous communities or geo-political regions still actively colonized or living under occupation (the Americas, Puerto Rico, Guam and other American-occupied Pacific outposts, and the Occupied Palestinian Territories), postcolonial theory cannot reach the critical depths necessary to undo the effects of European imperialism on Indigenous identities. In these contexts, there are still political, geographical, social, and legal fights—and in some instances, armed conflicts—that are underway because of the colonialist enterprise. For that reason, many writers from these and other contexts shy away from postcolonial theory and instead choose a discourse of *decolonization* and/or *anti-colonialism*. Rather than defining decolonization as a theory that examines social dynamics, I use the definition Waziyatawin Angela Wilson and Michael Yellow Bird do: "intelligent, calculated, and active resistance to the forces of colonialism that perpetuate the subjugation and/or exploitation of our minds, bodies and lands, and . . . engaged for the ultimate purpose of overturning the colonial structure and realizing Indigenous liberation."[60]

Decolonization or anti-colonialism as a discourse, in my view, is much more subjective and is a process very much underway in the present. Indigenous voices writing or speaking about decolonization express the everyday lived experiences of people living under colonial occupation. Decolonization in North America requires a different form of resistance than decolonization movements in African countries that won independence from England, France, Germany, and Belgium in the twentieth century. The ruling elite of *Kanata* or the US no longer identify as European and most Settlers and Arrivants are going nowhere. So, this book assumes that colonization is *fait accompli* in the Americas, and Indigenous discourse across disciplines is necessarily decolonial in nature. I do not argue for a revolution of geopolitical independence, but for a revisionist revolution, a revolution where both Indigenous and non-Indigenous communities understand our shared histories, and embrace and privilege the unique position of Indigenous Peoples in the Americas.

One

The Realities

Getting to "The Facts on the Ground"

WHEN I WAS co-chair of the core group of the World Council of Churches' Palestine Israel Ecumenical Forum from 2007 to 2010, the Palestinians in our consultations would often speak of "the facts on the ground" when talking about life in the Occupied Palestinian Territories. This would happen whenever the conversation turned to something theoretical or historical and strayed from the actual oppression of Palestinians living under occupation. At the time, I didn't always fully understand what they meant. But the term "facts on the ground" has taken on new significance for me as I have researched and reflected on the contemporary context of Indigenous Peoples in North America. For my Christian Palestinian friends, what matters more than arriving at a perfect theological or political position on the situation is their lived realities—the facts on the ground. I don't intend to discuss the Israel-Palestine conflict here, although there are striking similarities between the Palestinian people's quest for justice and that of Indigenous Peoples in Canada. The facts on the ground for Indigenous people are continued oppression, racism, alienation, eradication, and silencing of the Indigenous by the worst- and sometimes best-intentioned of people. And yet it is surprisingly difficult to document the details of this reality.

The Government of Canada regularly compiles statistical data on Indigenous Peoples in *Kanata* on the Statistics Canada website; however, it is still difficult to find comprehensive analysis that compares the lived experience of Indigenous Peoples and Settlers. For example, the most recent data (as in previous study periods) on select health indicators for Indigenous Peoples, collected between 2017 and 2020, looked at "First Nations people living off-reserve, Métis, and Inuit."[61] The summary digest of the study states that "Residents of Indian reserves, health care institutions, some remote areas and full-time members of the Canadian Forces were excluded."[62] According to 2016 Census data, an estimated forty percent of Indigenous people in Canada live on reserves.[63] If their experience is excluded from the data, it is difficult to paint a holistic picture of health and well-being for Indigenous people in Canada.

Perhaps the most significant work documenting the reality of Indigenous-Settler relations in *Kanata* was published in 1996. After half a decade of community, governmental, and nonprofit consultations, the Royal Commission on Aboriginal Peoples (RCAP) issued its report. The mandate of the Royal Commission was to study the evolution of the relationships between Aboriginal peoples in Canada, different levels of Canadian governments, and Canadian society as a whole. The report of the commission was over four thousand pages long, divided into five volumes, and spanned sixteen areas of priority with hundreds of recommendations. It laid out both immediate and long-term resolutions that required governmental and societal action. The report set out a twenty-year plan and recommended increasing funding for Aboriginal issues to $1.5 billion over the first five years of the plan, with an additional $2 billion over the next fifteen years, plus additional investments that would be needed in the long run.[64]

Appendix A of Volume Five of the report summarizes the recommendations from all volumes of the report. The recommendations are organized into broad categories with specific, measurable actions spelled out under each category. The broad categories include:

- That a renewed relationship between Aboriginal and non-Aboriginal peoples in Canada be established on the basis of justice and fairness;

- That the appropriate place of Aboriginal peoples in Canadian history be recognized;
- That the nature and scope of the injury caused to Aboriginal peoples by past policies in relation to residential schools be established and appropriate remedies be devised;
- That the nature and scope of the injury caused to Aboriginal peoples by past policies in relation to the relocation of Aboriginal communities be established and appropriate remedies be devised;
- That the nature and scope of the injury caused to Aboriginal peoples by past discriminatory policies in relation to Aboriginal veterans be established and appropriate remedies be devised;
- That historical treaties be fulfilled;
- That the federal government establish a process for making new treaties in a way that replaces the current comprehensive land claims process;
- That the federal government prepare a new Royal Proclamation for the consideration of Her Majesty the Queen to supplement the Royal Proclamation of 1763, and set out a bilateral nation-to-nation relationship between First Nations and the Canadian state;
- That a companion act of government be created to support the treaty process;
- That all governments in Canada recognize that Aboriginal peoples are nations vested with the right of self-determination, and that the jurisdiction of the Aboriginal governments be clarified;
- That there be formal dual citizenship — that is, all Aboriginal peoples are citizens of their Aboriginal nation and citizens of Canada;
- That the collection of data and statistics from Aboriginal communities be improved by Statistics Canada;
- That there be created an Aboriginal Parliament;
- That federal and provincial governments conform to a set of prescribed principles related to land bases and how they are considered in the treaty making / fulfilment process;

- That First Nations land base be expanded in the interim and the long term;
- That Aboriginal governments have access to and jurisdiction over natural resources, including mining, oil and gas, water, forests, land, hunting, trapping, fishing, harvesting, outfitting;
- That there be established economic development agreements that include culturally appropriate economic development institutions and adequate access to land and resources for economic development;
- That there be a focus on Aboriginal business development;
- That child and family welfare is a fiduciary responsibility of Aboriginal nations and their communities;
- That good health is essential to Aboriginal nations' well-being;
- That there be a commitment to adequate housing for Aboriginal peoples;
- That education is a core area for the exercise of Aboriginal self-government and that Aboriginal education requires significant investment;
- That there be created a national comprehensive inventory of historical and sacred sites;
- That museums and cultural institutions adopt a set of ethical guidelines for dealing with Aboriginal peoples;
- That support be put in place for increasing the participation of women, youth, elders, Métis, peoples of the North (Inuit and Innu), persons with disabilities, and urban Aboriginal peoples in governance and health and healing initiatives;
- That there be an immediate First Ministers meeting with Aboriginal leaders within six months of the release of the report;
- That the federal government establish an Aboriginal Peoples Review Commission to monitor the progress of the government on the recommendations of the report;
- That there be a commitment to public education on Aboriginal issues;

- That representatives of Aboriginal peoples be included in all planning and preparations for any future constitutional conference convened by the government of Canada.[65]

To date, Canada has acted on fewer than a handful of the recommendations in the twenty-year plan outlined by the report. This may be, in part, because the report itself is difficult to access, and its findings were never paid much attention in public discourse. I remember most media coverage at the time focused on the cost of the commission, and very few political leaders or community organizations engaged seriously with its reports at all. Except for the major work undertaken from 2008 to 2015 by the Truth and Reconciliation Commission on Indian Residential Schools and the creation of a $350 million Healing Fund, very little has been accomplished. The realities of life for Indigenous people are not widely understood. A poll conducted shortly after the release of the RCAP found that "nearly half of the Canadians polled thought that Indian reserves had similar standards of living and well-being as non-Aboriginal communities."[66]

The statistics, when summarized properly, prove otherwise. Sociologists Dan Beavon and Jerry White show that despite relative gains over a twenty-year period from 1981 to 2001, registered Indians in Canada still lag behind the general Canadian population in almost every measure.[67] Over twenty years have passed since these statistics were collected, and it's nearly impossible, given the changes to *Kanata's* census, to replicate what they would look like in 2011 and 2021. We do know, however, that life expectancy has decreased for Indigenous Peoples in *Kanata.* It plunged by 6 years between 2017 and 2021.[68]

		1981	**1991**	**2001**
Life expectancy at birth (years)	**Registered Indians**	65.7	70.6	72.9
	Canadian Population	75.6	77.9	78.7

		1981	1991	2001
Proportion Completed High School or Higher	Registered Indians	33%	55%	57%
	Canadian Population	60%	68%	75%
Proportion Completed Grade 9 or Higher	Registered Indians	60%	72%	83%
	Canadian Population	80%	86%	90%
Average Annual Income (2000$)	Registered Indians	$6,840	$8,243	$10,094
	Canadian Population	$16,554	$20,072	$22,489

While Beavon, White, and Spence's edited volume on developing a new and more insightful human progress index (the "community well-being index"[69]) gives some overview of the larger realities of Indigenous communities, most other remotely helpful scholarship relating to the lived experiences of Indigenous Peoples in *Kanata* since the RCAP report is too narrowly focused. Academic articles and books each address only a single issue or subtopic and barely scratch the surface of the bigger context. While the above table appears to show some significant gains across all measures, I argue that these gains have occurred *despite* Canada's failure to take meaningful action since the Royal Commission and are due mainly to the efforts of Indigenous Peoples to survive—and sometimes thrive—under colonization.

It is shocking that as we approach the thirtieth anniversary of the RCAP, a report of this depth and weight is still hardly acknowledged outside of academic circles. I believe there are two reasons for this. First, it appears that the report was simply too overwhelming for many people, and second, it did not purport to solve the "Aboriginal problem" as perceived by Settlers and the Settler colonial government. Instead, the commission challenged *Kanata* to avoid the assimilationist approach to Indigenous Peoples taken by Settler society:

> The analysis we present and the avenues of reconciliation we propose in this and the other four volumes of our report do not attempt to resolve the so-called "Aboriginal" problem. *Identifying it as an Aboriginal problem inevitably places the onus on Aboriginal people to desist from "troublesome behaviour"* [emphasis added]. It is an assimilationist approach, the kind that has been attempted repeatedly in the past, seeking to eradicate Aboriginal language, culture and political institutions from the face of Canada and to absorb Aboriginal people into the body politic—so that there are no discernible Aboriginal people and thus, no Aboriginal problem.[70]

The dominant society in *Kanata* has continued to resist a renegotiated and renewed relationship as outlined by the commission. Its recommendations have been ignored by policymakers and Canadian society alike, and Indigenous "issues" have slipped into the background of Canadian consciousness, only rising to the surface when Indigenous "troublesome behaviour" surfaces in the form of revelations about the traumas of Indian Residential Schools, Murdered and Missing Indigenous Women and Girls, and statistics on Indigenous (un)health, unemployment, and educational gaps.

The assimilationist perspective can be clearly seen in the writings of Canadian political scientist Tom Flanagan. Since the release of the RCAP report, Flanagan has stridently argued that a new orthodoxy of thought on Indigenous issues has taken hold among those who had influence over Aboriginal policy in Canada. He feared that this new orthodoxy would afford Indigenous Peoples unique rights separate from the dominant society in *Kanata*.[71] In his book *First Nations? Second Thoughts* he responded to the RCAP report:

> Canada will be redefined as a multinational state embracing an archipelago of aboriginal nations that own a third of Canada's land

> mass, are immune from federal and provincial taxation, are supported by transfer payments from citizens who do pay taxes, are able to opt out of federal and provincial legislation, and engage in "nation to nation" diplomacy with whatever is left of Canada. *This is certainly not the vision of Canada I had when I immigrated in 1968* [emphasis added] and decided to become a Canadian citizen in 1973; I doubt it's what most Canadians want for themselves and their children.[72]

Flanagan goes on to problematize Indigenous Peoples by stating, "Perhaps the damage to Canada would be tolerable if it meant that aboriginal peoples would escape from the social pathologies in which they are mired to become prosperous, self-supporting citizens."[73] Although he seems unable to see it, these challenges are exactly what the Royal Commission was trying to address. While Flanagan has been thoroughly critiqued,[74] his unabashedly assimilationist views represent a view still shared by many Canadians: "aboriginal people need to acquire the skills and attitudes that bring success in a liberal society, political democracy, and market economy. Call it assimilation, call it integration, call it adaptation, call it whatever you want: it has to happen."[75]

Flanagan is an easy target for those of us whose understanding of the world and colonialism in the Americas differs from his, but it is important to understand how commonplace this perspective is in Canadian society. And Flanagan's views are not the only way Indigenous voices are silenced. In 2013 Cree health researcher Michelle Reid listed some of them in an opinion piece on Rabble.ca titled, "How not to respond to Indigenous experiences of racism in Canada":

1. Don't bring up your own experiences of discrimination.
2. Don't claim you have more important things to worry about than racism.
3. Don't argue that some racism is worse than other racism.
4. Don't act like not being racist is a burden on you in particular.
5. Don't try and trap them in a racism logic puzzle.
6. Don't trot out your "Native friend" stories.

7. Don't use ignorance as a shield.
8. Don't use history as a scapegoat or an excuse.
9. Don't refuse to acknowledge that you might be living in a racist society.
10. If you realize you're wrong, don't refuse to apologize.[76]

Reid's list describes a reality experienced by Indigenous people daily and reveals the rhetorical smoke-and-mirrors techniques used to obscure the realities and histories of Indigenous experiences.

Flanagan suggests that Aboriginal people need to "escape" social pathologies, presumably through their own efforts. But what his perspective doesn't acknowledge is the constant pressure pushing against every aspect of life for an Indigenous person. Before Indigenous people can increase their capacities in any sustainable way, socialized obstacles must be removed. Examples of socialized obstacles include lack of access to education, primary health care, lack of access to capital, inadequate infrastructure, and corporations and governments who break promises made verbally or in a contractual, legal sense.

The reality is that Indigenous Peoples are required to walk multiple paths simultaneously. We must heal, overcoming the social pathologies that are rampant in our communities, and we must continue to assert our rights in the face of ongoing colonization. *Kanien'kehaka* scholar Taiaiake Alfred describes the internal struggle:

> Distracted from our goal, we wander a forest of frustration living inauthentic lives that make us easy prey for those who would enslave us . . . The present crisis reflects our frustration over cultural loss, anger at the mainstream's lack of respect for our rights, and disappointment in those of our own people who have turned their backs on tradition.[77]

In my view, the issue is even more complicated and more critical than Alfred acknowledges here, though I think he knows this. The distractions that send us wandering in the "forest of frustration" are the consequences of centuries of colonial oppression. Psychologists Eduardo and Bonnie Duran explain:

> Once a group of people have been assaulted in a genocidal fashion, there are psychological ramifications . . . the psyche reacts by internalizing what appears to be genuine power—the power of the oppressor . . . At this point, the self-worth of the individual and/or group has sunk to a level of despair tantamount to self-hatred. This self-hatred can be either internalized or externalized.[78]

Internalization and externalization of oppression in Indigenous communities are highly visible as social pathologies: rampant health problems, drug and alcohol abuse, paedophilia, spousal abuse, child abuse, sexual violence, gambling addictions, homelessness, bad credit, the inability to hold a job, social awkwardness, and poor education, to name a few. These are the statistics-backed topics that one finds in the scholarly articles on Indigenous life in contemporary North America. The most well-known study of the legacies of intergenerational traumas is probably Gabor Maté's *In The Realm of Hungry Ghosts: Close Encounters with Addiction*, although the past decade has seen a significant increase in related studies. As Duran and Duran argue, "Without a proper understanding of history, those who practise the disciplines of applied social sciences operate in a vacuum."[79]

When historian Geoffrey York wrote *The Dispossessed: Life and Death in Native Canada* in 1989, he noted:

> Strangely, most Canadians are better acquainted with the history of native people in the eighteenth and nineteenth centuries than they are with the unsavoury realities of recent years. Canadians know that the early Settlers and governments took land from the Indians, but it is easy to feel detached from those events of long ago. It is more difficult to deny responsibility for the misguided policies of the twentieth century. And so the ugly events of recent history are buried behind a wall of illusion—the illusion that progressive thinking and improved attitudes have brought fair treatment to Canada's native people.[80]

This illusion that York describes is the subject of my political critique. That illusion is what allows the contemporary political injustices of Indigenous reality to persist: an illusion held by non-Indigenous people that progressive thinking and improved attitudes have brought fair treatment to Indigenous people. Duran and Duran have examined how postcolonial theory can aid in the healing of the oppressed, and although changing with the emergence of Critical Whiteness Studies, very little has been written about the psyches of the dominant society and the ways in which colonialist thinking is still thriving in North America.

The Royal Commission recognized the paradigm shift that must take place for true equality to exist and for justice to be served to those who have been colonized. They argued that to let go of the past and move forward, two things must happen. First, Settler society must *acknowledge* the injustices of the past. Echoing York, the commission wrote:

> Widespread ignorance of the history of dispossession has made it increasingly difficult for non-Aboriginal people to admit the need for restitution. Unfortunately as Aboriginal people have gained strength in the struggle for their rights there has been a rising tide of opposition among non-Aboriginal people with an interest in maintaining the status quo. Their watchword is "equality": everyone should be treated the same, regardless of deprivation and disadvantage or the origins of these conditions. Acknowledgement and a genuine desire to make reparations are essential prerequisites of a renewed relationship of fairness and mutual respect.[81]

Secondly, the Royal Commission asked for a new Royal Proclamation to be issued by the sovereign, then Queen Elizabeth II of England. The commission suggested that consultations to prepare for this new proclamation—which would invoke the Royal Proclamation of 1763 as the legal basis for Indigenous relationships with the Canadian state—could commence within six months of issue of the RCAP report. Nearly thirty years later, no action has been taken by the sovereign or Canadian government. While neither England nor

Kanata recognize the actions (or inactions) of the state as acts of colonization, this lack of movement on Indigenous justice issues is colonialist in nature.

The concept of colonialist thinking was introduced by Albert Memmi[82] and later expanded by semiotician Walter Mignolo.[83] In my introduction, I explained how colonialist thinking is often understood as overt colonialism or as intentional acts of oppression or genocide. But there is a passive form of colonialist thought—one that Reid describes well in her Rabble.ca article—that is based on ignorance. Mignolo explains that the idea of place is a colonial construction: that the idea of a place is only a mirage that serves the colonizer/creator of that space. Mignolo most clearly lays this out in his concept of the "ontology of continental divides" in *The Idea of Latin America.*[84] However, it is in Memmi's *The Colonizer and the Colonized* that I find the best exploration of the psyche of the colonizer/colonialist.[85]

Memmi defines both Settlers and the descendants of Settlers who accept the status quo of colonization as colonialists. He argues that "accepting the reality of being a colonizer means agreeing to be a nonlegitimate privileged person, that is, a usurper. To be sure, a usurper claims his place, and, if need be, will defend it by every means at his disposal."[86] I believe this drive to defend nonlegitimate privilege creates a huge cognitive dissonance in North American society. To ease that dissonance, the Settler must prove that colonization does not exist or does not privilege them. The alternative may well be self-hatred in the oppressor. (In the oppressed, self-hatred is manifested as nihilism).[87] "In other words, to possess victory completely, [the oppressor] needs to absolve himself of it and the conditions under which it was attained," Memmi goes on to say. "This explains his strenuous insistence . . . He endeavours to falsify history, he rewrites laws, he would extinguish memories—anything to succeed in transforming his usurpation into legitimacy."[88]

Much like a downward spiral for the oppressed in which the negative effects of nihilism cause increased self-hatred, Memmi identifies the self-defeating process of self-hatred in the oppressor as a Nero complex: the more the oppressor oppresses, the more he hates the oppressed:

> His disquiet and resulting thirst for justification require the usurper to extol himself to the skies and to drive the usurped below the ground

> at the same time . . . the more the usurped is downtrodden, the more the usurper triumphs and, thereafter, confirms his guilt and establishes his self-condemnation.[89]

The ultimate end of this cycle of oppression is the complete eradication of the oppressed, at least the eradication of any visible presence of the oppressed. In the North American context, Andrea Smith identifies the manifestation of the usurper's role as the logic of genocide in white supremacy. She writes:

> A . . . pillar of white supremacy is the logic of genocide. This logic holds that Indigenous Peoples must disappear. In fact, they must *always* be disappearing, in order to enable non-Indigenous Peoples' rightful claim to land. Through this logic of genocide, non-Native peoples then become the rightful inheritors of all that was Indigenous—land, resources, Indigenous spirituality, and culture. Genocide serves as the anchor of colonialism: it is what allows non-Native peoples to feel they can rightfully own Indigenous Peoples' land. It is acceptable exclusively to possess land that is the home of Indigenous Peoples because Indigenous Peoples have disappeared.[90]

There is a finality to Smith's argument here that is important to note. Smith takes colonization as complete, rather than holding out hope for post-colonial liberation. In *The Colonizer and the Colonized*, Memmi wrote from the context of Algeria, where colonization was still relatively recent, in contrast to more than five hundred years of Settler colonialism in North America. His answer to the condition of colonization was to seek national liberation. In a post-Arab Spring world one can—as Memmi has in his most recent works—argue the merits of national liberation and of the post-colonial regimes that continue to replicate colonialist privilege and oppression. But in the North American context, Smith's words ring true: the supposed disappearance of American Indigenous communities means colonization is *fait accompli*.

In the North American context, I believe that colonization was ultimately successful and is finalized. A form of paternalism in which any aid from the oppressor to the oppressed is presented as a gift rather than an obligation[91] took root in the era of the residential and boarding schools, and colonialist privilege is safely ensconced in structures of stratified Whiteness in North American society.

This is why I support Tinker's argument that all Indigenous theology must be political theology. The fact is, Indigenous Peoples in our context *have not disappeared.* This results in a political problem. The RCAP report touched on over four hundred actions necessitated by this political reality. We must figure out what to do as a society when colonization is considered complete. There is little to no hope of a post-colonial existence for Indigenous Peoples, so attending to laws, policies, and rights is of paramount interest to both Indigenous and Settler/Arrivant communities.

Epistemology and Difference

Given the finality of the colonial context in continental North America—which includes American colonies like Puerto Rico, Guam, and American Samoa—we need new ways of examining the problem and working towards renewed relationships. By examining the epistemological differences between Indigenous and Western cultures we can gain insight into the strengths of multiple worldviews. Holding Indigenous epistemologies against Western epistemologies helps us to see the ways in which Western dualisms have created forms of knowledge that would otherwise just be considered normative.

Indigenous epistemologies are more comfortable with ambiguity and multiple concurrent realities. They do not need to eliminate Western conceptions of truth, but rather say: "Your reality is a truth, and there are many truths."

So far, there exists no discipline of "Indigenous epistemologies." In fact, only a handful of scholars of Indigenous descent have completed PhDs in philosophy, so it would be premature to attempt to develop a subdiscipline of Indigenous epistemologies within philosophy's subdiscipline of epistemology. However, there are scholars—mainly in philosophy, education, and curriculum studies—who are writing on epistemological questions.[92] The issues they raise, alongside other marginalized communities critiquing the strongholds of

Euro-Western philosophical traditions, can be woven together into a general presentation of epistemological perspectives that form a loose whole.

Indigenous epistemologies are part of a larger movement to decolonize epistemology. Mignolo writes that "Decolonizing epistemology means to decolonize naturalized principles on which knowledge is built, in disciplinary formations as well as in ideological discourses in the public sphere."[93] Like Mignolo and other Latine theologians and philosophers who are trying to decolonize epistemic privilege of dominant society in North America, Indigenous scholars also seek to articulate "a critical self-reflexivity that begins with an avowed and explicit identification of the locus of our knowledge and whose understandings we privilege, thus making evident where knowledge is being produced."[94] The parallels between Indigenous and Latine perspectives are very similar:

> [Latine] thinkers, aware of the ways in which the dominant society is ignorant of our experiences and ways of understanding, have a rich insight into how much self-ignorance affects us and affects the larger society. The dominant group, in contrast, being blind to its own privilege, has created an epistemic hegemony: an epistemic hegemony that makes it possible for those in the dominant group to ignore or disavow their epistemic privilege.[95]

Because, as I articulated earlier, there does not exist a body of research that constitutes a collected works of Indigenous epistemologies, chapter two will focus on the decolonial project identified by Mignolo as it relates to some of the epistemic hegemony argued by Isasi Díaz and Mendieta, and others. Rather than drawing on the extensive work of a particular group of scholars, I will instead draw together different Indigenous and Indigenist (including Latine) voices to decolonize some traditional tenets of Western epistemology. The aim is not to supplant Western epistemological conventions, but rather to liberate both Indigenous and non-Indigenous communities from epistemic hegemony by presenting alternative worldviews and showing how they affect our understandings of truth and reality. If Indigenous communities still suffer grave and multiple oppressions, that means that the dominant society is also suffering as the oppressive force. Indigenous perspectives can present a way forward that may be liberative to both Indigenous and non-Indigenous communities alike.

There is much public discourse, at least in the Canadian context, focused on reconciliation between Indigenous and Settler/Arrivant communities. I believe that deconstructing the epistemological differences that exist between different cultural groups is necessary before true reconciliation can occur. An Indigenous understanding of what constitutes truth and fact, how that understanding is employed in a societal context, and the richness and diversity it respects, can help us move towards reconciliation by teaching us to see that my gain as an Indigenous woman is not necessarily your loss as a non-Indigenous Settler/Arrivant. There are multiple ways of seeing the world; sometimes when different perspectives are perceived as competing, they simply aren't. Sometimes multiple things can be true at the same time.

If dialogue is the objective, then both Indigenous communities and the multiple iterations of Settler and Arrivant societies must commit to the task of dialogue for the sake of dialogue, for the sake of our society as a whole, and for the sake of a future where there is more equity, opportunity, and balance for all, based on a foundation of justice and decolonization. I will make this argument in more detail in chapter five through the lens of interculturalism.

Bearing Witness: A Decolonial Theology of Mission

When I finished my Master of Theology degree, I was convinced that there were postcolonial directions that missiology could and should take. In the conclusion to my thesis, I argued that David Bosch's concepts of humble boldness and bold humility[96] were ways of framing the impact that Christian mission could still have on the world, without some of the colonialist thinking that had plagued the churches over the centuries. Postcolonial discourse, when I first encountered it during my early years of graduate studies, was paradigm shifting. It was as if the subaltern voices that were speaking were speaking directly *to me*.

As my own scholarship has deepened, and I reflect on postcolonial contexts throughout the world, I have come to find strong academic allies in the works of other Indigenous scholars. Rather than fully promoting postcolonialism as my intellectual posture, I see myself as more of an ally in postcolonialism who remains firmly convinced of the need for a particularly decolonizing voice coming from Indigenous Peoples in the Americas. If we want to achieve liberation and decolonization in the context of Settler-colonization, we must demand Indigenous legal and human rights, redress for historical harms, and a relationship between Indigenous and Settler/Arrivant communities that is based on respect for the privileged place of Indigenous communities in colonized North America. By privileged place, I mean that our inherent rights and titles were never extinguished by colonization. And I believe that Indigenous political theology and missiology have an important role to play in this quest.

Here is another reason why a decolonized missiology is important. In *How It Is*, Viola Cordova's posthumously published volume of Native American philosophy, she recounts an episode from her childhood that showed her "how deadly serious Christianity was in the world that [she] had to live in."[97] Cordova describes how she asked one of her teachers, a Catholic nun, questions about the Bering Strait and why Cordova's own peoples' creation stories were absent from the biblical accounts of creation. The teacher became so agitated by the questions that she yelled at Cordova and told her never to come back because she was going to burn in hell.[98]

Like Cordova, I also believe that missiology can be deadly serious, and just plain deadly. It is, in my opinion, a matter of life and death. If theologies of mission can be used either as death-dealing forces of oppression, or to support a view of the divine which wishes us to have life and to have it in abundance, we must clarify which theologies we hold and why. While I will critique the shortcomings of theology and the churches, I do so as a Christian. My personal faith and my commitment to the way of becoming Christ-centred, cruciform, or Christ-like in discipleship is strong, and I believe that for all of the deadly blows Christianity and its institutions have dealt and continue to deal to the world Creator loves, there is life-giving potential in Christian faith that must also be honoured. And so, this book is a way for me to bear witness to my personal faith and do the work of evangelism to which I am called by Paul, in 2 Timothy 4.5: "As for you, always be sober, endure suffering, do the work of an evangelist, carry out your ministry fully."

In this I am very much inspired by the works of two missiologists in particular: Vincent Donovan and Jayakiran Sebastian. In *Christianity Rediscovered*, Donovan writes:

> Never accept and be content with unanalyzed assumptions, assumptions about the work, about the people, about the church or Christianity. Never be afraid to ask questions about the work we have inherited or the work we are doing. There is no question that should not be asked or is outlawed. The day we are completely satisfied with what we have been doing; the day we have found the perfect, unchangeable system of work, the perfect answer, never in need of being corrected again; on that day we will know that we are wrong, that we have made the greatest mistake of all.[99]

In a similar vein, Sebastian writes: "I have come to believe that we need to interrogate this concept and offer a theological critique of how [*missio Dei*] has played out in empirical terms, in order to provoke and stimulate other, possibly more productive and more relevant, ways of thinking and acting in this religiously plural and culturally globalized world."[100]

The place from which I wish to interrogate or query *missio Dei* as a concept, then, is from the seat of decolonial discourse. I have often echoed the words of my first professor of theology by saying "theology matters." American Indian studies scholar Jodi Byrd (citizen of the Chickasaw Nation) has a parallel (and complementary) position: "that colonization matters. For Indigenous Peoples, place, land, sovereignty and memory matter. In a world growing increasingly enamoured with faster, flatter, *smoother*, where positionality doesn't matter so much as how it is that we travel there, Indigeneity matters."[101]

Two

Indigenous Epistemologies: An Exploration

EPISTEMOLOGY HAS BEEN defined simply as the study of knowledge. The term comes from the classical Greek *epistēmē*, meaning understanding or knowledge. The discussion of what constitutes knowledge or the understanding of knowledge dates to the Platonic school, where scholars discussed how to define what constitutes "justified true belief."[102] Western philosophical traditions of epistemological enquiry have provided the basis for the economic and political worldviews that shape dominant society in both Europe and North America. The Western tradition(s) can serve to limit what is considered true, valid, or valuable.

In this chapter I will examine some of the historical approaches to the discipline of epistemology that influenced nineteenth and twentieth century theologies. I will then outline some alternative or decolonized theories of knowledge developed by Indigenous scholars. Since I will present Western and Indigenist thought as two contrasting worldviews, I will refer to epistemologies in the plural, recognizing that within these two broad perspectives (and, in fact, the myriad other epistemologies, globally) there are multiple schools of thought or traditions. My purpose here is missiological; my experience living in both Western and Indigenous spaces has allowed me to see where missiology can be liberated and expanded by incorporating Indigenist perspectives.

First, a quick note as to why I use epistemology as a vein of enquiry rather than "cultural difference." Although the phrase "cultural difference" is often used to explain the gaps between Indigenous and Settler societies, a dedicated study of epistemological difference is more tightly focused in scope. Culture encompasses knowledge, language, belief, art, morals, customs, etc., while epistemology is concerned primarily with ways of knowing.

The project of comparing Western and Indigenous epistemological perspectives may seem controversial to a Western mind. Epistemology is simply epistemology, one might argue. The question of "what is justified true belief?" ought to apply to every cultural background. Why offer another approach to epistemology based on culture? For millennia Western thinkers have been pursuing the discipline of epistemology without asking themselves whether their perspectives were limited. European thought—Anglo-Saxon thought in particular—has influenced theology. In all this, Indigenous ways of knowing have been excluded.

The question "what is justified true belief?" and its philosophical antecedents are useful insofar as they help us understand the dominance of Western thought. However, these are not the *only* perspectives. Epistemological enquiry may look different when approached by another culture. I realize this argument may open me up to the charge of relativism, and there may be some merit to that charge, but philosophies from China, the Indian sub-continent, and Africa are also starting to distinguish themselves from Western viewpoints, and an Indigenist view adds yet another perspective.

It is important to understand that when it comes to Indigenous philosoph(ies) there is no "textual corpus" from which to draw. There are just a handful of contemporary American Indian, Alaska Native, First Nations, and Métis scholars writing in the field of philosophy, building on even more scant traditions of Indigenous thought in the North American academy. Even though these scholars seek to represent—in most cases, and to varying degrees—a pan-Indigenous or Indigenist perspective, they are nevertheless writing from uniquely individual perspectives.

To examine some of the key differences between Western and Indigenous epistemologies, I will first lay out some of the key assumptions upon which

Western epistemologies are based, specifically the perspectives that have historically influenced theology. I choose to start with Western epistemologies since they are the hegemonic forces driving philosophical, theological, and other academic disciplines in the North American context. Indigenous epistemologies, as they have been developed within the contemporary academy, are comparative in nature, so summarizing Indigenist perspectives will be easier if there are some more traditionally established concepts to act as foils for Indigenous epistemologies. All Indigenous scholars writing in the academy are forced, to some extent, to conform to the language of the academy.

The Bases of Western Epistemologies

As far back as Plato, the Western philosophical tradition's focus on reason and rationality has limited epistemological concerns. "Epistemology, or the theory of knowledge, is driven by two main questions: 'What is knowledge?' and 'What can we know?'," John Greco wrote in his introduction to *The Blackwell Guide to Epistemology* in 1999. "If we think we can know something, as nearly everyone does, then a third main question arises: 'How do we know what we do know?'"[103]

In the first half of this chapter, I present some of the current schools of thought in epistemology and the classical foundations upon which they are built. This will allow me to show where there may be natural synergies or support for Indigenist perspectives within Western philosophical discourse. More importantly, however, it will show where there is incongruence between Indigenous and Western worldviews.

Carrying on from the Platonic and Aristotelian epistemological concern with the "ideally formed belief" (later referred to as the "doxastic ideal"), medieval philosophers such as Thomas Aquinas, believing that theology was *scientia*, an organized body of knowledge, retained the centrality of the doxastic ideal in the practice of theology.[104] According to philosopher Nicholas Wolterstorff, "Two ideas were central in Aquinas's adaptation of the Aristotelian concept of *scientia*. *Scientia* is a community enterprise; and in that community enterprise, the phenomenon of a proposition or argument being *evident* to a person plays a central role."[105]

I want to briefly address the role of community in the development of the concept of *scientia*. This is the one area in my survey of Western approaches to epistemology where I have found an important acknowledgement that belief, especially justified true belief, is both created by and limited to the community that holds it to be self-evident. Given the vast cultural disparities between Indigenous Peoples and Western civilization, it is not surprising that Western thinkers have believed that because justified true belief presents itself to be self-evident, it is therefore true. But if we examine how that belief became a dominant perspective, we can more clearly see the Western philosophical hegemony and free ourselves from it. I will come back to this later in this chapter.

The French philosopher René Descartes is generally considered to be the father of modern epistemological thought. Descartes presented a radical binary dualism that distinguished the mind as separate from and superior to the body. Descartes and other philosophers who came after him excluded the knowledge that is obtained from non-cognitive functions. Only knowledge gained through the cognitive functioning of intellect was valued. This binary dualism is expressed in the famous Cartesian claim "I think, therefore I am."

Descartes's epistemology is based on an experience of profound doubt and re-evaluation. In his "Discourse on the Method of Rightly Conducting the Reason and Seeking Truth in the Sciences," Descartes begins his first "meditation" by stating:

> Several years now have elapsed since I first became aware that I had accepted, even from my youth, many false opinions for true, and that consequently what I afterwards based on such principles was highly doubtful; and from that time I was convinced of undertaking once in my life to rid myself of all the opinions I had adopted, and of commencing anew the work of building from the foundation, if I desired to establish a firm and abiding superstructure in the sciences.[106]

Whatever it was that prompted such an intellectual upheaval, Descartes does not say, nor does he attempt to debunk his previously held beliefs one-by-one. Rather, he attempts to construct a system for understanding truth as a basis for knowledge. In the process he rejects the experience of the body apart from the mind.[107]

Descartes further develops ideas about two forms of knowledge: *scientia* and *persuasio*. For him, *Scientia* is "true knowledge" in the vein of Plato's "justified true belief." One obtains knowledge to form a belief so strongly that it cannot be undermined by any stronger belief: We are certain of what we know, but we are also certain why we know that understanding to be true.[108]

Persuasio is a form of conviction—as opposed to "true knowledge"—that is based on strong belief but measured against the possibility that the belief could be disproven. Descartes identified *persuasio* as a conviction held when there remained some reason that might still cause one to doubt the belief.[109]

This distinction between *scientia* and *persuasio* sets up a hierarchy of knowledge upon which "justification of truth" is then developed. *Scientia* is preferred over *persuasio* because there is no room for doubt; it is justified and therefore absolute. This line of thinking assumes that doubt is negative and should therefore be abolished if at all possible. By abolishing doubt, the thinker proves that he is not dreaming, says Descartes.

Ultimately, Descartes constructs a systematic process for eliminating doubt to establish truth. Belief and doubt are inversely related in Cartesian thought: as belief increases, doubt decreases, and vice versa. This reveals, again, a radical binary dualism in which belief or knowledge is good and doubt is bad. Western philosophy since Descartes has continued in its pursuit of *scientia* as superior to *persuasio*, valuing knowledge that is beyond question and disembodied—that is to say, does not come from physical experience but only from cognitive reason. This is also the basis for Cartesian morality. Cartesian philosophy continues to be both vigorously critiqued and staunchly defended.

John Locke, one of Descartes's main interlocutors, based his own philosophy on some of Descartes's assumptions: First, that knowledge is only made up of cognitive thought since the mind has no other object than its own ideas, and second, that knowledge consists alone in the connection of an agreement between (or disagreement and repugnancy of) any of our ideas.[110] Like Descartes, Locke attempted to establish a systematic approach to determining what correctly defines truth in the process of determining knowledge. And, like Descartes, Locke based his philosophy on a negation of bodily experience.

Locke's approach is more constructive than Descartes's (i.e. not founded on the eradication of doubt). For this reason, Locke does not attempt to devalue the body in relation to knowledge; he simply does not acknowledge the body at all. For him knowledge is about ideas; reason is about the discovery of knowledge by enlarging our field of enquiry and by regulating our assent to ideas. Locke organizes reason into four "degrees": "The first and highest is the discovering and finding out of truths; the second, the regular and methodical disposition of them, and laying them in a clear and fit order, to make their connection and force be plainly and easily perceived; the third is the perceiving their connection; and the fourth, a making a right conclusion."[111] Locke's conceptions of knowledge and reason and Descartes's definition of truth as unshakeable conviction became the basis for epistemology in Western thought.

The work of Scottish philosopher David Hume has had a profound effect on epistemology. Hume earned a reputation in the academy as a life-long atheist and was maligned to some extent because he rejected theology as a basis for epistemology, opposing medieval philosophers, who were very much concerned with the metaphysical dimensions of epistemology. Hume dismissed as "nonsensical" Descartes's concerns about proving whether one was awake or dreaming. In *An Enquiry on Human Understanding*, Hume made plain his thoughts that his philosophical predecessor had been led astray:

> But as, after all, the abstractedness of these speculations is no recommendation, but rather a disadvantage to them, and as this difficulty may perhaps be surmounted by care and art and the avoiding of all unnecessary detail, we have, in the following enquiry, attempted to throw some light upon subjects from which uncertainty has hitherto deterred the wise, and obscurity the ignorant. Happy if we can unite the boundaries of the different species of philosophy by reconciling

> profound enquiry with clearness, and truth with novelty! And still more happy, if, reasoning in this easy manner, we can undermine the foundations of an abstruse philosophy, which seems to have hitherto served only as a shelter to superstition and a cover to absurdity and error![112]

Hume dismissed such distractions and focused instead on approaches to defining reason using the scientific method of empiricism. Hume's approach marked a departure from both Descartes and Locke and established a firm demarcation between the theological and the scientific methods.

Since the scientific method has become a way of continuing to exclude non-dominant voices in the academy, it is worth examining Hume's epistemological thought more closely. Hume argued several important theses. Perhaps his most famous idea is the Copy Principle, which first appeared in his lesser-known work *A Treatise of Human Nature.*[113] The Copy Principle describes a causal relationship between simple impressions, simple ideas, and complex ideas. By reproducing simple impressions and forming copies of them, a thinker arrives at more complex ideas. These ideas are then re-examined and influenced by other ideas. While at first glance it may appear that by rejecting traditional metaphysics Hume is reintroducing a more embodied approach to defining truth and reason, his epistemology is still very much limited to cognitive interpretations of events.

A second important concept put forward by Hume is the necessity of definitions. In *An Enquiry Concerning Human Understanding* Hume concludes that mathematical solutions in reasoning are too lengthy and cumbersome, and that metaphysics is too ambiguous: "The chief obstacle, therefore, to our improvement in the moral or metaphysical sciences is the obscurity of the ideas and ambiguity of the terms. The principal difficulty in the mathematics is the length of inferences and compass of thought, requisite to the forming of any conclusion."[114] According to the Copy Principle, one cannot *think* anything one hasn't *felt.* In order to "fix" as a truth what began as a simple impression and was subsequently developed into a thought, it is necessary, Hume argued, "to fix, if possible, the precise meaning of these terms [power, force, energy, or necessary connexion], and thereby remove some part of that obscurity."[115] This philosophical imperative to establish definitions has contributed to the ideology of scientific empiricism that has developed during the last two centuries.

Immanuel Kant took Hume's arguments for scientific empiricism even further. Kant wrote his *Critique of Pure Reason* following Hume's criticism of Cartesian metaphysics. Kant went on to critique Hume's scientific empiricism in his *Critique of Practical Reason*. Kant argues three important points: 1) reason is the arbiter of empirical truth (i.e. truth that is established via the journey from impression to complex idea); 2) the role of reason in science is to determine the principles that determine scientific enquiry; and 3) the limits of reason must be defined.[116] It is the third point that has received the most philosophical attention, so I will briefly explore this line of his thought.

What I consider to be important in terms of Kant's influence on philosophy in general and epistemology in particular is the line he draws between mathematics and philosophy. Kant writes: "The exactness of mathematics rests upon definitions, axioms and demonstrations. I shall content myself with showing that none of these, in the sense in which they are understood by the mathematician, can be achieved or imitated by the philosopher."[117] This distinction is then used to argue for an *a priori* limitation of the philosopher's reason, especially regarding the transcendent. Kant claimed that, in the fields of theology and philosophy, men (I keep this gendered term since in Kant's time these vocations were pursued almost exclusively by men) had been grandiose in their estimation of their own mental capacities. He argued against Cartesian metaphysics and its theistic assumptions since any argument about the existence of a divine being could not be justified using the mathematical and philosophical methods that had been developed. Since justification of belief is one of the core precepts of epistemology, Kantian thought has presented one of the most important epistemological self-critiques in Western thought.

Kant argues that "in spite of the plainest and most urgent warnings men still allow themselves to be deluded by false hopes, and therefore to postpone the total abandonment of all proposed attempts to advance beyond the bounds of experience into the enticing regions of the intellectual world."[118] Rather than using experience to broaden intellectual engagement, he instead uses it to limit thought to what can actually be completely justified both through scientific method and causal justification. While previous thinkers on truth and knowledge might have been inaccessible because of the focus on the metaphysical, Kant renders too much thought as completely un-reason-able and therefore unable to be true.

The nineteenth to mid-twentieth centuries saw the emergence of several different philosophical movements as they concerned epistemology. Specifically, there was dialogical interaction between pragmatic theorists and correspondence theorists. The leading pragmatic theorists were Charles S. Pierce, John Dewey, and, most notably, William James. The central argument of pragmatism was that the finer distinctions in belief only matter insofar as they affect action and behaviour in the world. This occurred through a process of belief-formation, application, experimentation, and observation. James further refined the theory to argue that belief only mattered at the level of individuals and individual choice.

The last philosopher I wish to highlight in this chapter is Hans-Georg Gadamer, in particular his book *Truth and Method.* While Gadamer doesn't represent the idealist approach of the philosophers I have examined so far, his work tends to open spaces that overlap with Indigenist thinking. Indigenous philosopher Viola Cordova draws on Gadamer's work extensively. Gadamer's prominent voice in twentieth century hermeneutics has encouraged other modernists to resist the postmodern turn to subjectivity and relativism. The Australian philosopher Jeff Malpas writes:

> Trained in neo-Kantian scholarship, as well as in classical philology, and profoundly affected by the philosophy of Martin Heidegger, Gadamer developed a distinctive and thoroughly dialogical approach . . . that rejects subjectivism and relativism, abjures any simple notion of interpretive method, and grounds understanding in the linguistically mediated happening of tradition.[119]

Among Western epistemologies, Gadamer offers an even more narrow process for determining, not only knowledge and truth, but also the way in which information is interpreted. Influenced by Plato's *Dialogues*, Gadamer favoured dialogue as a method of philosophical and hermeneutical enquiry, and he placed a high value on historicity. "[H]istory does not belong to us; we belong to it," he wrote in *Truth and Method*.

> Long before we understand ourselves through the process of self-examination, we understand ourselves in a self-evident way in the family, society and state in which we live. The focus of subjectivity is a distorting mirror . . . *That is why the prejudices of the individual, far more than his judgements, constitute the historical reality of his being.*[120]

Gadamer argued for the rehabilitation of what he called "legitimate prejudices."[121] Legitimate prejudices were those he considered constitutive of all human understanding, but other prejudices were simply mistakes made from haste and error. He based his argument on what he considered the fundamental question for his hermeneutics: "What distinguishes legitimate prejudices from the countless others which it is the undeniable task of critical reason to overcome?"[122]

I note that Gadamer's argument has the unintentional effect of continuing to silence subaltern voices, or, at the very least, placing upon them the burden of justifying why their experience should be considered truth rather than a "prejudice." If it is a prejudice (according to Gadamer, we all have prejudices), then its legitimacy must be argued, although it is still epistemologically less than something that is reasonably understood to be true in the normative (i.e. dominant) context. This is why it is important to consider the role that power plays in epistemological arguments. When we make assumptions about what is considered a legitimate prejudice and what is not, we risk committing injustices, either wittingly or unwittingly. In attempting to answer his own questions, Gadamer concluded that one legitimate prejudice was the role of tradition in history. This was proven, he argued, "by the fact that the great achievements in the human sciences almost never become outdated."[123] He illustrated this idea further:

> A modern reader can easily make allowances for the fact that, a hundred years ago, less knowledge was available to a historian, and

> he therefore made judgements that were incorrect in some details. Overall, he would still rather read Droysen or Mommsen than the latest account of the subject from the pen of a historian living today. What is the criterion here? Obviously, the value and importance of research cannot be measured by a criterion based in the subject matter. Rather, the subject matter appears truly significant only when it is properly portrayed for us . . . Modern historical research itself is not only research, but the handing down of tradition. We do not see it only in terms of progress and verified results; in it we have, as it were, a new experience of history whenever the past resounds in a new voice.[124]

While this idea does not represent the totality of Gadamer's epistemology, this prejudice in favour of historical authority has profound implications for Indigenist thought in the academy.

In summary, here are four of Western epistemology's guiding principles that diverge in important ways from Indigenous epistemologies. The first is dualism. Dualism is implicit in Western thought: good vs. bad, right vs. wrong, knowledge vs. doubt, man vs. woman, fact vs. fiction etc. The second is the concept of truth as an ultimate subjective reality and of justification as the means by which belief in the truth is obtained. The third is the linear, causal progression of thought as articulated in the Copy Principle and the causal networks of knowledge presented by Hume and Kant. And the fourth is the privileging of historical authority and tradition as justifiable, as argued by Gadamer, despite the subsequent emergence of new information.

This is not an exhaustive list of the differences between Indigenous and Western epistemologies, but rather four places where two different worldviews contrast with each other. I will now outline some Indigenous approaches to these issues, after which I will conclude the chapter with an argument as to why both Western and Indigenist views are important for epistemological approaches to the humanities in the twenty-first century.

The Bases of Indigenous Epistemologies

Indigenous communities have had their own discrete epistemological perspectives and systems of thought for as long as Western philosophers have been contemplating questions of truth and knowledge (if not before). Until the late twentieth century they have not been included in the academy. In the introduction to his book *Tsawalk: A Nuu-chah-nulth Worldview*, theorist Richard Atleo highlights this point. He quotes Clement C.J. Webb, in *A History of Philosophy*, who writes that civilization begins with "leaving off telling tales."[125] Atleo writes that the "theory of *Tsawalk* not only begins with these 'tales,' or origin stories, but also depends on these 'tales' both as the foundation of knowledge about the state of existence and as a guide for its interpretation."[126] In other words, from an Indigenous viewpoint, truth and fiction cannot be so easily divided.

The academy's understanding and acceptance of Indigenous epistemologies is at a nascent stage and by no means can Western and Indigenous epistemologies be discussed as if they were on equal footing. What existing Indigenous voices can offer, however, are some different starting points from which we can develop Indigenist worldviews. While I include Indigenist perspectives from outside of North America, I focus mainly on the North American traditions that are familiar to me and most closely related to my own.

In his essay "What Coyote and Thales Can Teach Us: An Outline of American Indian Epistemology," Brian Yazzie Burkhart outlines the differences between Western and Indigenous epistemological bases. Burkhart uses the archetype of Coyote as philosopher in Native American legend. Coyote often loses his sense of himself and his place in the world because he is too busy wondering about things and about how they really work. Plato told the story of the Greek thinker Thales who was ridiculed for being so eager to know what was happening in the heavens that he fell down a well, unaware of what had been at his feet. The difference in the two approaches, Burkhart says, is that:

> Plato uses the story of Thales to make clear what philosophy *is*. He explains that "[the philosopher] is unaware what his next-door neighbour is doing, hardly knows, indeed, whether the creature is a man at all; he spends all his pains on the question, what man is, and what powers and properties distinguish such a nature from any other" (*Thaeaetetus* 174). The stories of Coyote, conversely, are meant to show Coyote's mistakes. Like Thales, Coyote has forgotten the simple things. He has forgotten his relations. He has forgotten what is behind him and at his feet. When Coyote behaves this way, he always finds trouble. He is mocked in these stories because he is behaving the wrong way. The stories are meant to show us how not to act; they show us what philosophy is not, and not, as in the case of Plato and Thales, what it is and ought to be.[127]

Indigenous epistemologies are less concerned with metaphysical principles and more concerned with the simple everyday things around us. Burkhart also points out that there is significance in how questions are framed. Unlike Western epistemologies that presume unquestionable truths guide our lines of enquiry ("i.e., we can ask any question we desire and in any way we desire, and the answer will remain the same"),[128] Indigenous epistemologies hold that "how we act is not merely a response to stimuli," but rather, "the way in which we ask questions (the way in which we act towards our relations) guides us . . . to the right answers, rather than the other way around."[129] In other words, the thinker is guided by the limits of questioning rather than the limits of reason. I experienced this myself. As a young adult I was often told that you could not learn with idle hands; it is only when your hands are busy that you learn. You did not sit down to interview your Elders. It was more appropriate to be busy with them, and then you could talk. I received some of my most important lessons about our culture and about our peoples' traditions while sewing, washing dishes, or walking through the woods to gather traditional medicines with my Elders. You must be busy to learn; asking direct questions is inappropriate. Spending time working with someone is an invitation to let them teach you something about life.

Furthermore, in our culture it is common to use a declaratory statement rather than a command to achieve a desired outcome or action. Viola Cordova writes about announcing to her children: "Your room is messy!" or "The garbage can is full!" rather than telling them to clean up their room or empty the garbage.[130] She explains:

> My value system is built around the concept of a human being that says that all humans are equal and therefore deserving of respect. Who am I to command another to do my bidding? . . . Just as one cannot tell another person what to do, one can also not ask for anything. To ask for something is to imply an inability to be independent. To ask for anything is to imply to the person asked that he or she has failed to be perceptive to the other's existence or needs. Telling another what to do implies a position of command that no human being, or *no real human being*, would presume to take upon him- or herself.[131]

Meaning is not shaped by enquiry into the human mind, but rather by participating in right action. In other words, epistemology begins in theological anthropology. Human relationships are much more focused on the other—the needs of the other and the other's inherent right to be—and less focused on the internal enquiry presented by Western philosophers.

This difference is often evident when researchers are working with Indigenous Peoples. When a non-Native person asks an Indigenous Elder certain questions, Burkhart writes, "Native elders will respond by saying, 'We don't talk about those things,' or 'It is bad to talk about those things.'"[132] Linda Tuhiwai Smith highlights this cultural misstep in *Decolonizing Methodologies*, in which she examines Western approaches to research and the implications of that research for Indigenous Peoples. In the opening of her book, Smith writes, "the word itself, 'research,' is probably one of the dirtiest words in the Indigenous world's vocabulary. When mentioned in many Indigenous contexts, it stirs up silence, it conjures up bad memories, it raises a smile that is knowing and distrustful."[133] Smith responds with a set of research protocols that are more reflective of the relationship-based epistemological positions of Indigenous Peoples. Specifically, she articulates a set of values that are prescribed by Māori for researchers in cultural terms:

1. *Aroha ki te tangata* (a respect for people).
2. *Kanohi kitea* (the seen face, that is, present yourself to people face to face).
3. *Titiro, whakarongo . . . korero* (look, listen . . . speak).
4. *Manaaki ki te tangata* (share and host people, be generous).
5. *Kia tupato* (be cautious).
6. *Kaua e takahia te mana o te tangata* (do not trample over the *mana* [life force] of people).
7. *Kaua koe e whakahihi to matauranga*[134] (don't flaunt your knowledge).

> These sayings reflect just some of the values that are placed *on the way we behave* [emphasis added].[135]

Brian Yazzie Burkhart argues that the limitations of asking questions as a research method relate to an Indigenous understanding of the moral universe. He writes, "The idea is simply that the universe is moral. Facts, truth, meaning, even our existence are normative. In this way, there is no difference between what is true and what is right . . . The guiding question for the entire philosophical enterprise is, then: what is the right road for humans to walk?"[136] This is perhaps one of the greatest points of contention between Western and Indigenous worldviews. If, from an Indigenous viewpoint, right action is more important than justified truth claims as the teleological goal of rational enquiry, then this chasm must be bridged before philosophical dialogue between cultures can happen. This can only be done by investing in intimate relationships where right action becomes discernable. Without such relationships true understanding will be limited.

Settler researchers may ask: "How can less knowledge be better?" According to Burkhart, this question is "partly a result of Western philosophy's incapacity to grasp the idea that certain things *should* not be known."[137] The idea that some things should not be known applies in Indigenous communities. There are powerful spiritual forces at work in some of our cultural practices that, much like Western theological concepts, can be used in constructive or destructive ways. For example, a hereditary chief from my hometown once taught me a healing song but gave me strict instructions not to teach it to a particular person who was not sober. No good would come of it if I did, I was told. One day I happened to be giving this person a ride in the chief's car when a recording of the song started playing on the sound system. Not recognizing the song, the person asked, "What song is this?" I responded that it was a beautiful healing song. "Listen to this part," I said, and I proceeded to play one part over and over again, rewinding and fast forwarding so they wouldn't hear the whole song, and I wouldn't have to explain that they wouldn't be given permission to learn it.

These cultural differences have resulted in many failed interactions between Indigenous Peoples and Settlers in North America throughout the last five hundred years. Western approaches to knowledge and research still cause Indigenous people to be objectified in scientifically empirical studies that are missing the relational element and that fail to respect boundaries around asking questions in an Indigenous context. Rather than seeing these boundaries as limitations on knowledge, Burkhart suggests that "our knowledge is not limited since we have as much as we should."[138]

While Western epistemologies are grounded in propositional knowledge—truth and justification, with the pinnacle being timeless truths—Indigenous epistemologies are grounded primarily in experiential knowledge guided by a moral universe in which we are co-actors with the divine and creation. According to the dominant Western view, justification of truth is seen as evidence for a truth claim. Even Western perspectives that claim pragmatic or common-sense confirmations of truth are grounded in the science of Cartesian logic.

This is counter to an Indigenous point of view. Whether we call Indigenous knowledge "experiential," "embodied," or "lived knowledge," Burkhart writes that "this kind of knowledge is not improved by adding abstract propositional form and is not capable of being justified in the foundational sense and seems to need no justification."[139]

Another epistemological difference between Indigenous and Western perspectives is the concept of a linear progression of time. I have written about this elsewhere,[140] but one of the best explications of Indigenous concepts of history and time can be found in Donald Fixico's *The American Indian Mind in a Linear World: American Indian Studies and Traditional Knowledge.*[141] Aside from the fact that Indigenous oral traditions do not satisfy Western philosophical requirements of truth and justification, they are also epistemologically different in that their function is primarily pedagogical and political. Native oral traditions are ways of explaining the moral universe. This is the central purpose of Indigenous epistemology, as Burkhart points out. Indigenous oral traditions are pedagogical in the sense that they teach communities central truths or values which are formative in right relationships with all of creation. They are political in the sense that they embody the consensus-based decision-making model that Fixico articulates in his description of "Indian thinking," which he describes as:

> visual and circular in philosophy. Imbedded in an Indian traditional reality, this ethos is a combination of the physical reality and metaphysical reality. Listening and observing the natural environment is essential to the Indian mindset. Decision making is responsive in nature due to considering all of the physical and metaphysical factors affecting one's life. Coming to a consensus is coming to a balance of all factors so that the right decision is the best decision for all concerned.[142]

Fixico goes on to say that "The power of story through the oral tradition is also explained [in] how all of this[143] transcends time, thus making time less relevant to the power of oral narrative told effectively."[144]

Many Indigenous cultures have strict ownership and protocols around the use of stories, preserving the tradition (rather than accuracy) in a way that honours its origins and purpose. Unlike Gadamer's valuation of history and authority, Fixico argues, an Indigenous perspective values the principle of right action in meaning making. The purpose in telling a story is not to present knowledge *a priori* or to justify *a priori* knowledge, but rather to define a right way of being in balance in the world and to synthesize a communal experience of what the right path of action should be.

Fixico's idea is supported by Cordova. She describes differences in how Indigenous and Western worldviews determine and define "stability." For Western thinkers, she says, stability is seen as a static, unchanging state. By contrast, stability to the Native American is "a balancing act" in a universe exhibiting many motions that will require different balances.[145]

Yet another epistemological difference relates to the Cartesian dualism upon which Western thought is based. Feminist philosophers have critiqued the mind/body dualism of Descartes, but Burkhart is concerned primarily with an individual/collective dualism:

> [T]he real Cartesian bias is the idea that knowledge can only be acquired and manifested individually, in or by the individual. The *cogito, ergo sum* tells us, "I think, therefore I am." But Native philosophy tells us, "We are, therefore I am." A Native philosophical understanding must include all experience, not simply my own. If I am to gain a right understanding I must account for all that I see, but also all that you see and all that has been seen by others—all that has been passed down in stories. What place do I have to tell you that your experiences are invalid because I do not share them?[146]

This points to a larger difference between Western and Indigenous thought; Western binary dualisms have been largely imposed on Indigenous communities in North America whom Settlers viewed as primitive and undeveloped, and whose worldviews they devalued. Philosopher Anne Waters argues:

> The maintenance of the rigid distinct boundaries of binary logic enables (though may not necessitate) an hierarchical value judgement to take place (e.g. mind over body, or male over female) precisely because of the sharp bifurcation. A nonbinary (complementary) dualism would place the two constructs together in such a way that one would remain itself, and also be a part of the other. In this way, a hierarchical valuing of one being better, superior, or more valued than another cannot be, or rather, is excluded by the nonbinary logic.[147]

This is the philosophical issue at stake: Western binary thinking insists that Indigenous epistemologies are inferior or incompatible with Western epistemology. From a Western perspective this may be so, but from an Indigenous perspective they can be complementary, adding to the whole of human philosophical experience. While Waters would acknowledge that the domination of Indigenous Peoples in North America by successive generations of Settlers has resulted in large gaps in our knowledge of the original ontologies and epistemologies of Indigenous cultures, she maintains that kernels of knowledge have remained. Just because many Indigenous Peoples have been eliminated or prevented from practicing philosophy doesn't mean we can't recognize their worldviews to be true or exercise an intuitive critique of the culture imposed on us as the dominant alternative. Waters writes, "the importance of order and balance, as well as proper (moral) behavior, are part of the cosmological understanding of our universe."[148] This perspective has been dismissed because it is often presented in romanticized ways by Indigenous and non-Indigenous scholars outside of the field of philosophy. However, the work of the growing number of Indigenous philosophers in the academy brings to light the ways in which this intuitive epistemological perspective can show the academy a different way of doing philosophy in a moral universe.

Ts'msyen lawyer Calvin Helin capably blends these two worldviews in his book *Dances with Dependency: Indigenous Success through Self-Reliance*. In the introduction, Helin recounts a solemn oath he took together with his brothers in front of their dying father that they would "stick together."[149] In his writing on Indigenous self-reliance, Helin observes that in Tsimshian culture the self is very communal:

> Although it certainly might be helpful if more remnants of Indigenous cultures were still in existence, we do not have to turn back the clock in order to find the still-pristine emotional legacy of our ancestors, stressing the importance of social interconnections and the necessary interdependence of families, Tribes or Nations. Or to recognize the value of self-reliance, high moral conduct, loyalty, self-sacrifice

> and leadership. This renewal must be done in a modern context in constructive partnership with the larger society.[150]

The nondiscrete, nonbinary nature of Indigenous thought has implications for another cultural misunderstanding that arises frequently between Native and non-Native scholars—namely, the question of "true" indigeneity.

For example, because of my white skin, because I, my mother, my brother, or my children do not have one hundred percent (or some acceptable percentage) "blood quantum" or the right kind of "Status" (as passed down by the father, according to Canadian law), we are somehow considered "less" *Haíłzaqv* than someone whose blood quantum is higher or whose skin is darker. Yet I have been told by my elders that regardless of who my father is, and regardless of who my son's father is, we are *Haíłzaqv* (the *haíłzaqvla* spelling of the anglicized "Heiltsuk").

Anne Waters's reasoning for nondiscrete nonbinary dualisms in Indigenous thought is based on transcultural studies of surviving Native languages in North America. She writes about moving towards an articulation of her own Indigenous ontology and epistemology:

> I then thought about static bifurcations of the discrete binary (bounded) dualities of essentialisms in contemporary feminist thought and recent race theory: male/female, masculine/feminine, man/woman; Black/White, Indian/non-Indian, Hispanic/not-Hispanic, Asian/non-Asian, etc. These discretely bifurcated and essentialized concepts suggested a way of being in the world that might run contrary to some Indigenist ontology we find remaining in American Indian languages. And the problem seemed to be not so much that "language has gone on a holiday," but rather, that deep structures of Indigenous thinking about ontological relations in the world conflicted with the discrete binary logic inherent in Euro-American reflection about relations in the world.[151]

She evokes the cry of Caribbean women in race theory who ask, "Why can't I be Black *and* Hispanic?" and quotes Indigenous literary critic Paula

Gunn Allen who asks, "Who are these people who want to control, through language use, who I am?"[152]

My late grandmother—who was White and adopted my mother—objected ever so politely to me identifying as solely *Haíłzaqv*. She would have preferred for me to identify as "bi-cultural" (it sounds so much more benign, doesn't it?). But my people have told me I am *Haíłzaqv*, and "We are, therefore I am."

Weaving the Two . . .

In her book *Reshaping the University: Responsibility, Indigenous Epistemes, and the Logic of the Gift*, Sámi scholar Rauna Kuokkanen recounts an experience she had in Vancouver at a talk entitled, "Making Space for Indigenous Voices in Education: Engaging in New Conversation." Kuokkanen was excited by the plenary presentations but dismayed—though not surprised—at how Indigenous responses from the audience were quickly quashed by hegemonic Canadian perspectives. The first person to respond to the plenary spoke about decolonizing Canadian history and the need to return to Indigenous connections to land and questions of land ownership. Next, "a young woman want[ed] to know what define[d] First Nations identity in 2004 because for her, it seem[ed] unavoidably bicultural, both Canadian and Aboriginal at once."[153] Before the speakers could respond, another woman in the audience jumped in to point out the ways in which her First Nations friend was different from mainstream Canadians, and proceeded to argue that we needed to provide adequate education for all and not to essentialize based on racial identity. "Then [came] the grand finale," Kuokkanen writes, "the classic hegemonic counter-narrative to anything Indigenous: We're all Aboriginal! We just need to know our own heritage and cultural roots to find out that all traditions are the same. Once we've done that, the spaces for Indigenous education automatically happen!"[154]

This type of cross-cultural conversation that derails productive conversation about Indigenous and Settler/Arrivant relationships by attempting to eliminate difference reveals the epistemological hegemony of Settler and Arrivant societies. Indigenous voices are silenced because they necessarily challenge the dominant political history of Canada and the United States. Important conversations about land are lost amid attempts to eradicate differences. In Christian or theological circles, this impulse is often supported by a restrictive reading of Galatians 3.28: "There is no longer Jew or Greek, there is no longer slave or free, there is no longer male and female; for all of you are one in Christ Jesus." Left unchecked, the dominant culture's hegemonic drive will continue to ensure that Indigenous epistemologies remain disproven, discounted, fictional, anecdotal, and "inappropriately subjective" in an academy that is dominated by an epistemology grounded in Cartesian thought.

In answering the question "Can We Know the 'Other'?" Kuokkanen refers to what Gayatri Spivak calls "Eurocentric arrogance of conscience . . . the simplistic assumption that as long as one has sufficient information, one can understand the other."[155] When we consider the fundamental epistemological differences explored in this chapter, we can see why Spivak calls this Eurocentric perspective an "arrogance of conscience." But the question "Can we know the 'other'?" remains important; the future of Indigenous and Settler/Arrivant relationships depends on it. And Indigenous epistemologies offer us a gift as we attempt to answer this question: We can avoid the binary dualism of "us" and "the other." As Cordova reminds us, "We must, as philosophers, not lose sight of the fact that the reason for exploring alien ideas is to expand our understanding of the diversity of human thought and not to expand our own specific ways of thinking so that they encompass all others."[156]

So, the purpose of examining Western and Indigenous epistemologies alongside each other is to strive for nonbinary and complementary ways of knowing. To what end, we might ask. I would answer that, given colonization's transformation of Indigenous communities and cultures to cycles of paternalism and dependency, it is vital that we identify these social dynamics to move towards true healing and reconciliation.

Three

Indigenous Theology and Mission: Mission from Below

The particular bondage of American Indian peoples presents peculiar difficulties for identifying an appropriate starting point for writing an American Indian theology. We are faced, on the one hand, with a broad spectrum of the rich diversity of Indian mythological expressions and other traditional narratives, forms of Indian spirituality, ceremonies, and structures of Indian societies. Each of the hundreds of Indigenous nations of North America has its own discrete cultural and social structures that would provide for a very interesting theological reflection and would capture the imagination of many a reader, perhaps especially readers external to the American Indian community.

On the other hand, the contemporary Native American experience of disintegration and alienation derives from the ongoing history of conquest, oppression, and poverty, with all of their ongoing consequences. Thus, two different expectations of an Indian theology function—one characterized by euro-american desires for the exotic other of Indianness as a New Age spiritual delectable, the other characterized by Indian poverty and need. If a theology is to be a part of a people's life-giving, life-sustaining social structure, it dare not just be interesting, especially just interesting to an external audience. Rather, a Native American theology must not only speak out of Native

> American experience and culture, but also speak to the contemporary reality of Native American existence.
>
> —*George Tinker,* American Indian Liberation: A Theology of Sovereignty

IN THIS CHAPTER I will take a closer look at four of David Bosch's concepts of mission that I singled out in my introduction for deeper theological engagement from an Indigenous perspective. But first I want to explore the history and development of the concept of *missio Dei* in ecumenical thinking and reflect critically on its continued importance to mission and missiological studies today from an Indigenous perspective. It is worth noting that although Indigenous Peoples are some of the most "missionized" in the world, the theologies and histories of mission outlined by Western missiologists hardly acknowledge the role of Indigenous Peoples, either as subjects, objects, or communities with their own inherent potential to interpret and to construct unique theologies.

A Brief History of *missio Dei*

Two prominent missiologists, David Bosch and Francis Anekwe Oborji, give historical summaries of the origin of the twentieth-century missiological construct of *missio Dei*. In *Concepts of Mission: The Evolution of Contemporary Mission*, Oborji writes that World War II "prepared the ground for the emergence of the missionary theory of *missio Dei* and of mission as liberating service to God's reign."[157] Bosch traces the concept back further, however, to the interwar period. In 1932 Karl Barth read a paper at the Brandenburg Missionary Conference identifying mission as an activity of God.[158] The following year, Karl Hartenstein articulated a similar line of thought in *Dei Mission als theologisches Problem,* and a German delegation to the Tambaram meeting of the International Mission Council (IMC) did the same in 1938.[159] Meanwhile, a growing awareness of the complicity of mission with colonialism and racism[160] alongside Christian unity as the basis for the Life and Work movement[161] (launched in Stockholm in 1925), set the stage for the acceptance and promotion of the concept of *missio Dei* in 1952 at the IMC Conference in Willingen, Germany.

Barth's concept of *missio Dei* was limited in the sense that it identified Christian reconciliation as the foundation of mission. This led other theologians to rethink human agency with respect to mission. If mission was re-framed as the activity of the triune God, what role did humans play? The IMC meeting in Whitby, Ontario in 1948 had as its theme "Partnership in Obedience," which, according to Oborji, sought to "define the relationship between the 'older' and 'younger' churches in such a way that the common goal of one mission remained in sight."[162] This story of the genesis of *missio Dei* is important because to this day many mainline Protestant churches still engage in a partnership model of global missions. In recent years, global voices from the margins have drawn attention to the fact that this partnership model remains paternalistic, with the old churches coaching new ones but seldom being transformed by them.

Oborji's origin story of *missio Dei* addresses the underlying theological assumptions of *missio Dei* in a way that other summaries—such as Bosch's in *Transforming Mission* or Philip Potter's entry on "mission" in the first edition of *The Dictionary of the Ecumenical Movement*—do not. In addition to "Partnership in Obedience," the IMC also used the slogan "Expectant Evangelism" which invited theological reflection on new directions for mission in which eschatology and history were used to define history. Oborji writes: "But which history was meant, and which understanding of history was to be used for the interpretation of missionary events? The differences of opinion on these questions resulted in two trends: the salvation-history model (understanding the personal redemptive activity of God) and the history-of-the-promise model (the Gospels as promise)."[163]

These two models have had great influence on the theology of *missio Dei*, the former more so than the latter. German Protestant missiologist Walter Freytag shifted the emphasis of mission from humans to God and offered an eschatological perspective of missiology rooted in God's own self-giving.[164] This eschatological perspective was developed into a soundly Trinitarian perspective at Willingen in 1952. Bosch summarizes it thus:

"The classical doctrine on the *missio Dei* as God the Father sending the Son, and God the Father and the Son sending the Spirit was expanded to include yet another 'movement': Father, Son and Holy Spirit sending the church into the world."[165] The new understanding of mission was that mission was not primarily an activity of the church, as it had been understood in earlier historical periods when the church sent its representatives to geographical regions, but rather it was seen as an attribute of God. Since Willingen this concept has been accepted by mainline Protestants, Eastern Orthodox, and later evangelical Christians.[166]

The fact that *missio Dei* gained wide acceptance after 1952 does not mean that it has gone without challenge or without presenting further challenges to missiological discourse. Bosch and Oborji write that *missio Dei* was introduced to save mission from secularization. Both recognize that this effort failed. Instead, the secularization of church action became the defining characteristic of mainline Protestant mission. Many Christians—Europeans in particular—blamed America for what they saw as a dilution of *missio Dei* to include the whole world and to concern itself with secular development and relief work (as opposed to the missionizing work of winning souls for Christ). This was, perhaps, because the World Wars caused an accelerated rate of human suffering and pain on such a global scale, followed by rapid advances in industrial and communication technologies which had wide-reaching consequences for global and local economies.

Bosch concludes that "[d]evelopments like these have prompted [people such as Dutch theologian Philippus Jacobus] Hoedemaker to challenge the usefulness of the *missio Dei* concept,"[167] because it reduces potentially contradictory theological positions to relativism. This is an understandable critique but one that Bosch argues against, and one that can also be addressed by postmodern and postcolonial theologies. In the end, both Bosch and Oborji conclude that despite the arguments for and against *missio Dei*, and despite unintended consequences such as the secularization of mission, it has liberated the theology of mission from the notion that any church or human being could be the author or bearer of mission.[168] Mission is the work of God alone.

Missio Dei also opened new possibilities for ecumenical dialogue by making the Protestant concept of mission more compatible with both Roman Catholic and Orthodox theologies and ecclesiologies, which are historically more Trinitarian than Protestant lines of thought. Prior to Willingen, Orthodox theologians had struggled to discuss mission at all with Protestant churches and theologians.[169] But the articulation of *missio Dei,* which emphasized the internal sending of the Triune God, allowed for further dialogue on mission between Orthodox and Protestant theologians.

One criticism that the concept of *missio Dei* has received is that the underlying theology is too abstract. Hoedemaker and others have expressed concern that *missio Dei* is relativistic and lacks meaning and direction for people. True, there is no clear consensus on what *missio Dei* actually *means.* Since Willingen, several ecumenical statements have expanded on the concept of *missio Dei* in ways that are helpful, though not without further problems. A series of statements—"Mission and Evangelism: An Ecumenical Affirmation" by the World Council of Churches (1982);[170] the Urban Rural Mission statement (1986); "Mission in Christ's Way: Your Will Be Done" (1989); and "Together Towards Life: Mission and Evangelism in Changing Landscapes" (2012) by the World Council of Churches' Commission on World Evangelism and Mission[171]—put flesh on the bones of the concept of *missio Dei* in ways that attend to the concerns of the world but still avoid charges of secularization and relativism. During consultations in preparation for the drafting of "Together Towards Life," the World Council of Churches (WCC) attempted to be attentive to the shifting demographics and concerns of churches in the Global South. The explosion of internet and mobile phone technologies has allowed churches around the world to document and share their struggles, stand in solidarity with each other, and advocate for each other. Churches in the Global North have been forced to listen more attentively to voices from the Global South. That said, there remains much in these statements that assumes the perspective of the Global North as the normative one.

The World Council of Churches' 2012 statement, "Together Towards Life," reveals an ecumenical movement that is still unsure of what these shifting paradigms mean. For example, the statement acknowledges that mission was once understood as "a movement taking place from the centre to the periphery, and from the privileged to the marginalized of society,"[172] and now "people at the margins are claiming their key role as agents of mission and affirming mission as transformation."[173] But while the statement recognizes that the roles of a sending church in the Global North and a receiving church in the Global South have, in many ways, been reversed, the statement merely poses questions about what this shift might mean rather than articulating a transformed missiology: "If there is a shift of the mission concept from 'mission *to* the margins' to 'mission *from* the margins,' what then is the distinctive contribution of the people from the margins? And why are their experiences and visions crucial for re-imagining mission and evangelism today?"[174] The subsequent sections of the statement focus on economics and environment, which is not surprising given the programmatic focus of the WCC since 1982, but contain little indication that the voices *from* the margins have explicitly transformed the ecumenical experience of the dominant churches.

"Justice, Peace and the Integrity of Creation" was the name of an ecumenical program of the WCC that attempted to put *missio Dei* into practice, yet that the program existed at all belies the contradictory nature of *missio Dei.* Although *missio Dei* is meant to change our understanding of mission from something humans do to something God does with human participation, it is still easy for churches and theologians—myself included—to talk about *missio Dei* as if it is something that humans *do*. Not only that, but I believe we still tend to preach louder than our actions—a tendency the ecumenical movement has held onto since the Third General Assembly of the WCC. As J.C. Hoekendijk names in *The Church Inside Out, we* have not liberated ourselves in ecumenical discussions from the constraints of what the WCC named from the Third Assembly on as "responsible risk"—naming the theological need to be prophetic that gets tempered by an overly cautious approach to action, fortified by our attachment to the status quo.[175]

Specifically referring to the sacrament of communion in his missiology, Hoekendijk writes, "The order for the celebration of the eschatological Sacrament of Communion must as a matter of course be an *eschatological order:* that is to say, open-ended and so structured that we can have this order 'as if we did not have it.' That is now clear. We can shut off nothing to the front of us, as if we could dispose of the future in any way."[176] He goes on to identify, with quite some wit, the ways in which the church of his time stayed stuck in its past, despite intentions to do otherwise:

> More difficult for us will be to deal with that plot against the future, that widespread conspiracy, which wants to leave everything as it is. The clever politics of the ostrich, which always leads us to put our head into the traditional sand ("we don't see anything new"); the fervent marking of time that is so reassuring ("we're progressing nicely, aren't we!"); and also that ingenious invention that we have copied from an American egghead: every day he takes off in his plane and sets his course so as to land where it is still yesterday. If I am not mistaken, this figure has quite a few followers in our circles. You can see it on a rather large scale: we take off in 1960 with a whole cargo of slogans about renewal and projects for the future; one would say we were bound to go in the right direction; but we still manage to set our course so as to land, for instance, about 325 (*Corpus Christianum*), or around 800 (parochial system), or precisely in 1517 (Reformation). You can see it in all possible ways, on a small scale also: for instance, we go searching for a *new* song (as we say) and then set course for the Bach airport, or just manage to make an (emergency?) landing on Gregorian soil.
>
> No, we can only really enter the new world if we dare, quite deliberately, choose tomorrow (and this means that if necessary we must deliberately choose against today and yesterday).[177]

This is still painfully relevant in the second decade of the twenty-first century.

I want to turn here to some early twenty-first century critiques of *missio Dei* that question its continued usefulness. Challenges that come from African and Asian contexts are important since they offer other contextual views of mission that have developed in partnership and consultation with Western traditional views of mission but without the same intellectual dependencies or obligations. Theologies and missiologies from non-Western contexts have successfully advocated for their own cultural and epistemological priority to be relevant in their own contexts.

Theologians in Africa, Asia, and Latin America have challenged the concept of *missio Dei* with the goal of ensuring that the work of mission remains grounded in the material realities of the people. This critique of *missio Dei* aligns with the socio-economic analysis presented by liberation theology. South African missiologist Willem Saayman writes:

> Precisely because of [Jesus's] solidarity with the poor and oppressed, God brings the liberating message of his good news to the rich and powerful also. This is so because it is an illusion for them to imagine that they can be free and enjoy peace while they are oppressing and exploiting others, whether directly or indirectly, whether by commission or omission.[178]

Both poor and rich are liberated for the sake of all. Indigenous theologies echo this concern, but with a broader lens that includes all of God's created order and challenges the idea of human beings as the starting point for reconciliation; God's kingdom intends that each *being* should have life and have it in abundance.

Critiques of *missio Dei* from the Global South take into consideration the interconnectedness of all aspects of life: environmental, political, social, religious, and intellectual. While European critiques of *missio Dei* have focused on the charges of secularism and relativism, communities in the Global South have maintained more balanced perspectives that integrate both material and transcendent realities. That said, critiques from the Global South may not have gone far enough to save the concept of *missio Dei*. Some contemporary scholars question its relevance. Philip L. Wickeri questions whether, in light of advancing secularization in the West, *missio Dei* is still useful;[179] Christopher Duraisingh advocates instead for a reclamation of a Franciscan theology of *concursus Dei,* or divine accompaniment;[180] and Jayakiran Sebastian applies an explicitly postcolonial lens to his reading of *missio Dei* from a South Asian perspective and suggests that we might understand it as *missio humanitatis qua intinerarium in Deum* (loosely translated as "mission as humans seeking to know God").[181]

It is important to acknowledge that the International Missionary Council (IMC) and churches in the Global North adopted the concept of *missio Dei* as a way of de-coupling evangelization from the "civilizing mission" of mainline Protestantism in the late nineteenth and early twentieth centuries. This must be celebrated. Yet, as Duraisingh, Sebastian, Wickeri, and others point out, the concept of *missio Dei* does not fully account for the lived realities of communities on the margins. More critical approaches to theologies of mission are needed that engage in power analysis and address the needs and sufferings of human and non-human beings without losing sight of the transcendent or the unique nature of Christian faith.

Jayakiran Sebastian, writing from the context of post-colonial India, presented a paper at a WCC consultation on mission held in Breklum, Germany in 2002. He suggested that:

> A re-examination of the *missio Dei* is necessary, because what is needed today is a mission paradigm that affirms our mission *to* God. Having gone through the consequences of theological thinking regarding the mission *of* God, and having explored human responsibility in this task, a reversal of the direction in trying to take seriously the human experience of both variety and difference in God/divinity, and what this means for the question as to whether there can ever be an understanding of a *common* mission of humankind, becomes an urgent theological task.[182]

Much like Indigenist thinkers, Sebastian argues for a move away from *missio Dei* as either the mission *of* God or mission *to* God. It is not that one concept is right and another is wrong. Instead, what is needed is a frank admission that, despite the good intention inherent in emphasizing mission as being *of* God, and the attempt to free (or perhaps cleanse) mission from colonization, nevertheless humans are still very much part of the missiological picture. So, Sebastian urges us to probe deeper:

> If mission is both a divine and a human enterprise, then what? Why use binaries? Can binaries become so intertwined that disentanglement is not only impossible, but also unnecessary? Why not talk about mission as "theandric"—not as the "result" of binaries being intertwined, but as the very nature of the being of the divine?[183]

This critique will be taken up more fully when I discuss Indigenous openness to multiple truth claims and rejection of binary dualisms.

Missiology from an Indigenous Perspective Must be Political

One of the exhortations offered by the Global South is that churches engaged in mission need to do a better job of addressing the material realities of people in ways that account for their contexts, their brokenness, and the many systems of injustice that oppress them. This critique is articulated well by some of the Asian theologians I highlighted in the section on *missio Dei*. More writings on mission from Asian perspectives are listed at the end of the book in the "For Further Reading" section.

There are no books from an Indigenous missiological perspective in the Americas save for the lone voices of George Tinker in North America and Nicanor Sarmiento in Peru.[184] But the Asian perspectives are well-summarized by Naga theologian Wati Longchar in an editorial in *The Journal of Theologies and Cultures in Asia*.[185] Under the historical colonial model of mission and conversion, Longchar argues, conversion was justified by the underlying colonial belief that modernity, Christianity, and rapid industrial advancement were inherently superior to traditional cultures. I would add that because Christianity was normative to European cultures, religious belief was deeply baked into European taxonomies of race. Longchar cites Tinker, who observed that the process of conversion resulted in four cultural disorientations: new converts were removed from their traditional communities; they were prohibited from rethinking their conversion and returning to their communities; they were forced to do physical labour to support the work of the missions and the military governments that supported them; and they were required to relinquish all aspects of self-governance.[186]

According to Longchar, since the colonial era Christian mission has developed through three stages: civilizing mission (bringing so-called civilization to people); charity mission (objectifying the poor and helpless *other* in need of charity); and development mission (developing communities that are supposedly undeveloped).[187] Longchar uses *missio Dei* in an implicit way to provide a basis for a re-envisioned missiology for Asia in the twenty-first century. He writes: "Christian witness and mission are about bringing healing, wholeness, and new life into the lives of individuals, communities, and nations. Breaking down barriers, seeking justice and dignity for all, building community, enabling reconciliation and peace among all peoples are at the heart of mission."[188] Any form of mission that does otherwise, he argues, is a betrayal and counter-witness to God.

Like Tinker, Longchar believes that "the churches in Asia need a transformative mission. Mission in Christ's way is God's mission amidst people in pain . . . This cannot be attained without justice. It involves struggle for transformation of a social system that ensures social, economic, political and cultural justice."[189] (I add gender and sexual orientation to Longchar's list.)

This is why a twenty-first century missiology from an Indigenous perspective needs to be political.

Responding to Charges of Retribution and Relativism

Many Western mission theorists (mainly Europeans, though some North Americans as well) have responded to this re-envisioning of mission by concluding that a people centred mission will take one of three paths. It will perpetuate the colonial model of the past, it will force contemporary Euro-Americans and Europeans to pay for the sins of their forebears, or it will make everything relative without a grounding in transcendent theology.

This Euro-Western hegemonic resistance to rethinking mission by people who are oppressed is not surprising. Most often, this is identified as a condemnation of Indigenous thought as "angry" and a perception that we seek retribution, not equity and restitution. I agree with Tinker that this resistance is simply denial as to the explicit and implicit ways in which dominant Western capitalist societies still oppress whole communities and nations of people. While the "colonial era," as we call it, may be over, colonialist thinking remains vigorous in the power structures of the world. Perhaps Western thinking is so bound to binary dualisms that any change in direction is automatically received as an attack against which the original position or idea must be defended.

But to be clear, the kind of justice we seek is not eye-for-an-eye retribution for harms of the past, but an acknowledgement of the ways in which colonialist thinking has hurt and continues to hurt Indigenous people. The justice we are seeking will not deny essential human rights and freedoms to the few individuals who are in positions of power and privilege, though it *will* challenge the power and privilege they hold. We seek this justice so that we all might heal. "Rather than ask whether immigrant descendants should have to pay the price for their ancestor's atrocities," Tinker writes, "a more constructive question might ask why American Indian heirs must pay the price for the oppression earlier euro-americans inflicted on our Indian ancestors." The healing of Native communities in North America is inextricably linked to the healing of non-Native communities. According to Tinker, the "liberation of euro-american peoples must be rooted in some sort of *systemic* confession and repentance with respect to their relationship with the native peoples of this continent."[190]

The charge of relativism is often used as another defense against a re-imagined missiology. This defensive argument appeals to the theological fallacy of Christian universalism. According to theologian John Franke, claims of universality are "no more than theology produced from the perspective of those who have cultural privilege."[191] Instead, he says, "the many parts of the church are called to participate together in a unity characterized by *interdependent particularity*. Each is a part, and only a part, of the embodied witness to the truth of the gospel made known in Jesus Christ."[192] This is both true and untrue from my perspective. Christian universalism presents troublesome and dangerous consequences if taken in a foundationalist "there is but one way to the Father" kind of a way. So, I wish to separate the concept of a *universal* Christianity from a *global* Christianity. A global Christianity would embrace the interdependency referenced by Franke, whereas a universal Christianity would not.

Bold Humility and Humble Boldness

Indigenous worldviews are often far more comfortable with the plurality of truth and experience than Western worldviews, and typically do not view the world in exclusive binaries. As an Indigenous theologian, I uphold two concepts when it comes to mission: *bold humility* and *humble boldness.*

Humble boldness describes a stance of humility that theologians (indeed, all Christians) should assume when witnessing to the life-giving power of the gospel in Christ. This is particularly important for Indigenous theologians because the history of missions in our communities has left modern Indigenous Peoples with justified feelings of anger and distrust towards Christianity in any manifestation. So, it requires humility in our boldness to speak the Good News of the Gospel, knowing that there are whole histories of oppression that impact our communities. Not only that, but we still are subjected to the romanticizing gaze of dominant Settler and Arrivant societies that expect every Indigenous person to speak on behalf of whole cultures in a way that would never be expected of a Western theologian. To continue to speak in this context requires humility as well.

Bold humility is a posture I believe the whole Christian community must assume to have corporate integrity. For too long Christianity has been entangled in the colonial enterprise, European taxonomies of race, and other systems of oppression. We must speak with humility, and to make that humility explicit in our proclamation of the Good News. Franke articulates it well:

> Our proclamation of the truth of the gospel must be bold in accordance with our confidence that God has indeed made known the divine will for creation and our conviction that in Jesus Christ the world is being reconciled to God. Yet at the same time, it must also be seasoned with humility due to our dependence on God; the limitations of finitude; our awareness of the differences among Christians concerning matters of faith, life, and practice resulting in the plurality of the Christian

community; and our understanding that in the present we know not in full but only in part even as we diligently seek to know and live out more of the truth and love of God.[193]

This is a wonderfully positive and hopeful way of interrogating and reimagining *missio Dei* that avoids radical binary dualisms and allows for diverse forms of flourishing within the context of an explicitly Christian faith narrative. I find this to be a fruitful interrogation of the concept of *missio Dei* rather than an outright dismissal.

Re-Viewing Missiology with Indigenous Eyes

I return now to the four missiological concepts I selected from Bosch to reframe them from an Indigenous perspective as part of my attempt to liberate mission from its Western hegemonic shortcomings. The four concepts are: *mission as church with others*, *mission as quest for justice*, *mission as liberation*, and *mission as theology*.

Mission as church with others

In *Transforming Mission*, David Bosch writes about the post-World War II paradigm shift from ecclesiological understandings of "church *for* others" to "church *with* others." "The church is the church only when it exists for others," wrote Dietrich Bonhoeffer from a Nazi prison. "The church must share in the secular problems of ordinary human life, not dominating, but helping and serving."[194] Subsequent theologians recognized this position as paternalistic. Instead, missiologist Theo Sundermeier and others promoted the idea of "church *with* others" to reflect the idea of equal coexistence.[195]

In this project of bearing Christian witness through my broken heart, I am at once naming the fallibility of the church and its theology while vociferously committing to its reform and renewal. I believe that the more we conceive of mission as church *with* others, the more this work of reform and renewal becomes challenging and necessary. It is messy work to be inclusive, to walk in solidarity with others, and to honour their perspectives and experiences as both valid and inherently worthy.

The work of being truly *church with others* is the business of interculturalism. What might intercultural theology look like? Various theologians have explored this question in recent publications including *Intercultural Theology: Approaches and Themes*, edited by Mark J. Cartledge and David Cheetham.[196] But an overview of these resources finds them lacking, both in diversity of perspective and depth of transformation. In the introduction to *Intercultural Theology,* Werner Ustorf writes: "The central aim of this book . . . is *to extend the conversation concerning the contemporary cultural conditions under which different theological accounts might be given.*"[197] The authors seemingly are trying to validate the themes and approaches of the *other*. Yet there is very little cultural diversity among the contributors. The book is dominated by Western perspectives concerned with definitions and how well other ideas measure up against those definitions. This benevolent collection seeks to explain something which it cannot itself embody.

Perhaps this oversight is psychological in nature. Ann Belford Ulanov, working in theology and psychology, explains that sometimes denial and projection can affect the sincerity and efficacy of apologies (and Cartledge and Cheetham's volume reads like an apology). She writes:

> While consciously both of us sincerely want to dissolve our dispute, unconsciously I want you to carry what I refuse to own. So I need you to continue to be an adversary—unreconciled—across the gap between us. If I leave that part in you, I have an unconscious need to control you, not reunite with you, because you bear a part that belongs to me that I must watch out for, manage. If we rectify our dispute then I must carry the repressed part of me I transferred to you.[198]

Ulanov is talking about individual interpersonal relationships, but society and the church are made up of individuals, each with their own psychological resistances to acknowledging complicity in oppression, especially when it comes to racism. The most common obstacle to change in a society marked by racism is denial. "Disavowal of our aggression does more harm than the aggression itself," Ulanov writes.[199]

First Nations in *Kanata* must deal with the collective wounds of colonialism, a type of multi-generational post-traumatic stress disorder that blocks further healing. Ulanov sees this as particularly problematic because past traumas can invade our present.[200] This is a problem for victims of trauma and also for members of the dominant society who repress their emotions about complicity in systemic racial injustice. A failure to feel these emotions, says feminist ethicist Linda Holler, causes dissociation from the erotic self—the self capable of *eros*, or intimate love. Holler writes: "Dissociation from the erotic self can happen as a result of war, accidents, malnutrition, child abuse, and other forms of violence . . . or pedagogical practices and ideologies bent on creating morally pure and obedient children."[201]

I would extend her analysis here to include pedagogical practices and ideologies that are bent on creating patriotic citizens who believe contemporary myths of nationalism built on colonization and manifest destiny. The dominant society in North America has been systematically taught to believe there is nothing wrong with the appropriation of First Nations land and to avoid responsibility for learning Indigenous histories of trauma. This prevents us from addressing our deepest historical political and social issues. Before we can achieve justice or true reconciliation, we must name these socio-political and economic injustices. Otherwise, we remain trapped in the psychological patterns established by colonization.

Church with others, therefore, requires a deeper type of emotional and psychosocial intimacy. To be intimately acquainted with the *other* is to know and participate in their struggles, to be transformed by interacting with them. Wati Longchar explains: "In today's context of Indigenous people, collective unified resistance is not an emotional or a charitable act, but it is a continual struggle for and commitment to the transformation of sinful social structure and the liberation of its victims."[202] The act of calling others into relationship and solidarity with us when we see mission as church *with* others is a rallying cry for justice. Longchar cites K.C. Abraham's definition of solidarity:

> Solidarity with the poor means entering into their struggle for justice . . . It is possible only if we enter into the life of others, especially the suffering, with openness and compassion. The spiritual resources for a new orientation should emerge from the collective experience of the poor and the marginalized . . . This is the only option left to us.[203]

This is why the next concept of mission I highlight in this work is *mission as quest for justice*. The presence of being *church with others* calls us to a posture of justice seeking. If we are to be church *with* others rather than simply *for* others we must necessarily be transformed by the lived experiences of injustice; we are called by our faith to seek justice, and that becomes a missional act.

Mission as quest for justice

In *Mission in Creative Tension* South African theologian Klippies Kritzinger writes: "The predicament of oppressed people is that they suffer from lack of power, that they are 'pushed down' by societal structures."[204] This results in a nihilism that manifests in self-hate and in what is starting to be named in Indigenous circles as "lateral wounding" or "lateral violence" (not unlike the nihilism identified by Cornel West in *Race Matters*).[205] Justice for Indigenous Peoples would mean creating a vision for the future that both forgives the harms of the past and at the same time insists on restitution and reconciliation. Every Indigenous scholar I have engaged with across all disciplines agrees that the only way Indigenous people (or any other oppressed group) can affirm their humanity and resist the temptation to nihilism is by combating systems of oppression. "[L]iberating mission is concerned not only with the conversion of the oppressed, but also of oppressors," Kritizinger writes.[206] Oppressors need liberation too; they have lost touch with their humanity because of their abuse of power and estrangement from the humanity of the oppressed. The first task for the oppressors in moving towards liberation is unmasking their hidden privilege and complicity in the status quo.

Kritzinger also believes in conversion. He witnessed the end of the Apartheid regime in South Africa and sees mission as the work of creating personal change in the lives of people.[207] But different people require different forms of conversion:

> As a result of the all-pervasive nature of *racism* in South Africa, to speak of the conversion of human beings in general is misleading: one has to distinguish between the conversion of Blacks and of Whites. At the same time, because of the pervasiveness of *capitalism*, one should also distinguish between the conversion of rich and poor people.[208]

He goes on to explain that the oppressed need to convert from the context of being *sinned-against*, whereas the oppressors need to convert from the context of *sinning*.

Much in the same way that Indigenous cultures prioritize dialogue over outcomes, the real work of mission occurs in the struggle. "As long as injustices prevail in society, Christians are called to combat them in the name of Christ. This is an integral part of prophetic Christian mission," Kritzinger writes.[209] From an Indigenous perspective, once these conversions have begun, mission will be on the road to liberation from its colonialist origins. A truly liberating theology of Christian mission will be based upon the decolonization of Indigenous and Settler thought and the relinquishment of Settler denial.

Mission as liberation

At the outset of this book I stated that missiology matters and theology matters. One of the critiques I hold, alongside others already mentioned, is that the concept of *missio Dei* is never fully defined in a way that becomes tangible, and consequently has lost some of the influence that its proponents hoped it might carry. And yet, the concept's flexibility in accepting multiple truth claims, I believe, is also a strength. In the introduction to *On Job: God-Talk and the Suffering of the Innocent*, Gustavo Gutiérrez reminds us that since biblical times Christians have believed that God is a mystery. "[I]t is important to keep in mind from the very outset that theological thought about God is *thought about a mystery*," he writes. "I mention this here because it influences an attitude to be adopted in the effort to talk about God."[210]

This is the attitude I believe is required when taking a liberationist approach. If we truly believe in mission as *church with others* and mission as *quest for justice*, respect for the divine mystery both cautions us and inspires us. We are cautioned against a type of self-assuredness and the necessity of making singular truth claims. At the same time, we are inspired to discover the truths present in the world around us through our relationships with the earth and with others. Gutiérrez goes on to say that just because something is hidden doesn't mean it must remain hidden:

> The "mystery" in this case must rather be expressed, not concealed; communicated, not kept to itself. E. Jüngel puts it well: in the Christian perspective, "the fact of having to be revealed belongs to the essence of mystery." . . . The revelation of the mystery of God leads to its proclamation to every human being: this is the special characteristic of the biblical message regarding mystery. Reflection on the mystery of God must therefore begin with God's resolve of self-communication to "all nations" (Matthew 28.19). The setting and requirements of the proclamation are fundamental presuppositions of any theologizing.[211]

We find revelation by entering into deep relationships with the world around us, through our mistakes, through the hurts and successes and pains and joys of ourselves and others. It is through solidarity and relationship with the other that we come to understand systems of oppression and injustice. The revelation comes to us through relationships and what was hidden from us is now no longer hidden. Gutiérrez suggests that:

> God is first contemplated when we do God's will and allow God to reign; only after that do we think about God. To use familiar categories: contemplation and practice together make up a *first act;* theologizing is a *second act*. . . Theologizing done without the mediation of contemplation and practice does not meet the requirements of the God of the Bible."[212]

The first act is contemplation and practice. Theologizing comes second. I have contemplated the political realities of my community and other Indigenous communities who face oppression. What does it mean for someone like me to follow a Christian path? While my own theologizing reflects the same "God of the Bible" who is at the source of Gutiérrez's theology, I do not often quote the Bible directly.

Hermeneutics is also part of the contemplation and action required by our faith, but I will leave that for another time. I would like to return to Kritzinger's argument that both oppressors and oppressed need to be converted for liberation to occur. Other theorists can help us define what liberation looks like.

Paulo Freire, the Brazilian educator who wrote *Pedagogy of the Oppressed*, believed that the purpose of education is to make students conscious of their political realities and to teach them to work for their own liberation from systems of oppression. Much like Gutiérrez, he argued that "[e]ducation is thus constantly remade in the praxis. To *be*, it must *become* . . . Problem-posing education is revolutionary futurity . . . since people do not exist apart from the world, apart from reality, the movement must begin with the human-world relationship."[213] The process of contemplation and reflection that leads to the revelation named by Gutiérrez is the same process of conscientization advocated by Freire.

The mystery need not stay hidden; Freire writes, "Any situation in which some individuals prevent others from engaging in the process of inquiry is one of violence. The means used are not important; to alienate human beings from their own decision-making is to change them into objects."[214] If we see mission as liberation then we must be vigilant to ensure that we are always seeking to uncover the mystery of the divine in all contexts and cultures. To become sure about mission or about the church or about God cements us into a place of inaction and death; static ideas turn into ideologies that stifle the impulse to liberate both oppressor and oppressed.

Philosopher John Caputo articulates quite concisely what happens when Christian mission is carried out from a place of certainty rather than humility and a justice-oriented curiosity for life:

> The church acts exactly as if it is self-authorizing, so that its work can only be interrupted and endangered were anyone to interfere, including

> Jesus himself, if he returned to see what is going on in his name. The church is not about to have its power questioned and its dogmas thrown into confusion by letting anything of that sort transpire. Having gotten used to the idea that the church defines and determines what Jesus stands for, and what Jesus would do, the church is not going to see its authority threatened by anyone, not even by Jesus himself. Whoever defies the teachings of the church by definition stands accused of heresy—and that goes for Jesus.[215]

The church, then, must be especially vigilant to ensure that revelation and conscientization are always active processes in the cycle of reflection and praxis that informs our theologies. This commitment to liberation must first and always come from a preference for those on the underside or the margins.

This is not a preference—as in liking one thing over another—but rather it is a *preferential option* or commitment to hearing the experience of the marginalized first. And not only hearing it but understanding it and becoming allied with it. Philosopher Enrique Dussel writes:

> The *Philosophy of Liberation* is a counterdiscourse, a critical philosophy born in the periphery (from the perspective of the victims, the excluded), which has the intention of being relevant on a global scale. It has an *explicit* consciousness of its peripheral and excluded character, but at the same time it has the intention and commitment of embracing and engaging the complexity of the world as a whole. It has emerged from and is committed to pursuing a conscious confrontation with European or North American schools of philosophy (both postmodern and modern, proceduralist and communitarian, etc.), which confound and even identify their concrete European origins with their unrecognized function as "philosophies of the center" throughout the last five hundred years.[216]

This means all our methodologies must consider the oppressed. The work of developing liberation methodologies first imagined by Freire and others is supported by a strong cultural undercurrent in the twenty-first century. Chicana cultural theorist Chela Sandoval argues that the methodology of liberation has resulted in a tradition of writers, thinkers, and activists across geographies and disciplines:

> It is no accident that over the last twenty years of the twentieth century new terms such as "hybridity," "nomad thoughts," "marginalization," "*la conciencia de la mestiza*," "trickster consciousness," "masquerade," "eccentric subjectivity," "situated knowledges," "schizophrenia," "*la facultad*," "signifin'," "the outsider/within," "strategic essentialism," "*différance*," "*raquache*," "performativity," "*coatlicue*," and "the third meaning" entered into intellectual currency as terminological inventions meant to specify and reinforce particular forms of resistance to dominant social hierarchy. Taken together, such often seemingly contending terms indicate the existence of what can be understood as a cross-disciplinary and contemporary vocabulary, lexicon, and grammar for thinking about oppositional consciousness and social movements under globalizing postmodern cultural conditions.[217]

This is hopeful. Given the tendency of humans to resist challenges to power and to struggle to acknowledge their complicity in systems of oppression, we must remain vigilant and continue to raise voices that conscientize both oppressed and oppressor, leading to the conversion of both sinned-against and sinner. This work of reflection and action to align with Indigenous Peoples and others at the margins—resulting in liberation—gives us the requisite basis for finally being able to theologize. This theologizing is the second act, possible only after doing God's will, according to Gutiérrez.

Mission as theology

Mission as theology is the final concept of mission I wish to highlight. It is, in my view, of paramount importance that mission as a theological discipline re-engages with other theological disciplines. Much missiological writing is concerned with reinforcing tradition and has missed many of the exciting theological developments of the late twentieth and twenty-first centuries. The most prevalent writers on mission, for the most part, concern themselves with ecclesiology, soteriology, enculturation, acculturation, syncretism, development in the Global South, social problems in the Global North, and the Trinitarian and/or Christological implications of mission. Yet there is much exciting and challenging scholarship happening in other theological traditions—specifically in constructive theology and biblical studies from scholars on the margins—that could profoundly influence how mission is defined and practiced in response to the challenges in today's world.

One such voice is that of the late Marcella Althaus-Reid, whose book *Indecent Theology: Theological Perversions in Sex, Gender and Politics*[218] challenged theological studies in critical and important ways. Lisa Isherwood, one of the editors of a recent essay collection in Althaus-Reid's honour,[219] describes her work as scandalous:

> The woman who is honoured [in this volume] . . . was a very complex theologian, a Quaker who carried more than one rosary on her person at all times and, when in London, often visited the British Museum to offer a gift to Bast, the cat goddess of the night; and also regularly attended the Church of Scotland. She was a theological materialist who resisted talk of metaphysics, hearing even talk of radical incarnation to be too vanilla for her tastes. She distrusted Mariology but had medals of Mary and saints around her neck along with a medal of Frida Kahlo. Marcella was a theologian who liked to ask the difficult questions and she certainly required that liberation theologies and feminist theologies look at themselves and face some harsh realities. Male liberation theologians were asked to look at their repetitions and sanitizations. She asked them to move their thinking away from the clean, male, shining and worthy Christs of the poor and to focus instead on lemon sellers, Xena and drag queens as the places where Christic realities may be lived out. With these as redemptive starting points she asked that they rework their theology in a more grounded and real way, a way that could not dodge political/economic and gendered questions rolled into one.[220]

I include this lengthy description to show what a unique person and theologian Althaus-Reid was. What scandalous good news this bold and creative theological maven brought to conversations on mission in the twenty-first century. Althaus-Reid revealed the heteronormative assumptions traditional systematic theology and biblical studies have made about the historical Jesus. She wrote: "The question of a Bi/Christ is related not to the sexual performances of Jesus, which we ignore. As far [as] we are concerned, Jesus may have been a transvestite, a butch lesbian, a gay or a heterosexual person. Heterosexual patterns of thought prevail in the narratives."[221] There are other theologians like Althaus-Reid who could radically transform missiology, but mainstream missiological discourse remains largely (to use her language) ultra-repressed and vanilla.

Another theological project that could offer much to Indigenous missiology is philosopher John Caputo's negative theology of "the weakness of God." Unfortunately, the field of missiology has not engaged with his work in any meaningful way. In his book *The Weakness of God: A Theology of the Event*, Caputo proposes that "the name of God is an event, or rather that it *harbors* an event, and that theology is the hermeneutics of that event, its task being to release what is happening in that name, to set it free, to give it its own head, and thereby to head off the forces that would prevent this event."[222] Defining the event of the divine as uncontainability, translatability, deliteralization, excess, evil, beyond being, truth, and time, Caputo seeks to deconstruct the ways in which the name of God is used under the guise of these conceptions to explain the event(s). Being trained as a philosopher before theologian, Caputo uses Jacques Derrida's approach to deconstruction: "I am tendering something in the spirit of what Derrida calls 'a non-dogmatic doublet of dogma,'" he writes. "This theology of the event lacks corpulent articles of faith, a national or international headquarters, a well-fed college of cardinals to keep it on the straight and narrow, or even a decent hymnal."[223] As a critical thinker and a philosopher, Caputo can cut through the power dynamics of theological discourse in ways that are helpful for the purpose of writing an Indigenous political theology.

Indigenous theologies are concerned with how systems of injustice affect physical bodies. Caputo is also concerned with bodies. He writes:

> The bodies we meet with in the kingdom are a singularly sorry lot: bodies laid low, afflicted with disease, bent by paralysis, racked with fever, withering away with leprosy, struck blind and dumb, or even lifeless . . . These bodies of flesh are attracted to Jesus by an almost natural gravitational pull, and he seems literally to be swarmed by them: they brought to him everybody like that. "[A]nd he cured them." Surely this is a case of like attracting like, because in the end Jesus ends up one of these bodies. The one who has become flesh becomes the most famous case of vulnerable, crucified flesh (which is also transformed and transfigured) ever to seize the Western world and imagination, which is why Mel Gibson's film *The Passion of the Christ* made so much money.[224]

This image of a fleshy and vulnerable Jesus requires us to rethink our understanding of the salvific work of Christ. What does salvation mean in the context of the physical abuses and horrible living conditions so many Indigenous people face? The urge to seek liberation and justice becomes more tangibly pronounced. This fleshy Jesus of Caputo hastens transformation: "Whenever Jesus swings into action, things are transformed; whenever he touches others or others touch him, they are transformed. If flesh means everything that is laid low and vulnerable, it also means, by the same token, inseparably and correlatively, everything that can be healed."[225] This is important for Indigenous Peoples who still face the highest per capita rates of poverty, incarceration, and dehumanization of any people group in North America.[226] Thomas King describes this grim reality more poetically:

> In order to maintain the cult and sanctity of the Dead Indian, North America has decided that Live Indians living today cannot be genuine Indians. This sentiment is a curious reworking of one of the cornerstones of Christianity, the idea of innocence and original sin. Dead Indians are Garden of Eden-variety Indians. Pure, Noble, Innocent. Perfectly authentic. Jean-Jacques Rousseau Indians. Not a feather out of place.

> Live Indians are fallen Indians, modern, contemporary copies, not authentic Indians at all, Indians by biological association only.[227]

Because "Live Indians" are left with all the baggage that comes with a fully accomplished colonization of a people and their land, the inauthenticity of the spectres who are biologically Indian but far removed from the romanticized imaginary of the Western mind challenges Settler/Arrivant communities to look at the brokenness of bodies in a way that must be incredibly uncomfortable. And yet, that is exactly what John Caputo argues for in *The Weakness of God*:

> One of the most interesting events, or laws of the event, in the New Testament, is that the out are in and the in are out. The characters in the kingdom are a cast of outcasts, of outsiders: sinners, lost sheep, lost coins, lost and prodigal sons, tax collectors, prostitutes, Samaritans, lepers, the lame, the possessed, the children. A list that we today could easily update: gays and lesbians, illegal immigrants, unwed mothers, the HIV-positive, drug addicts, prisoners, and, after 9/11, Arabs. Everyone who is outside, outlawed, outclassed—in short, everyone who is just plain out and should stay out of sight. Just the sort of folks who would send "For Sale" signs shooting up all over Christendom and who would send the Christian right scrambling for the exit signs at their next assembly (which schedules at least one session on their annual programs to denounce just about *everybody* to whom Jesus extended the kingdom).[228]

The intersection of the humour and poetics in Caputo's theology and King's history is a good place to situate an Indigenous theological concern.

The Open Ending

"Open Ending" is the conclusion to Catherine Keller's process theology text, *On the Mystery: Discerning Divinity in Process.*[229] Keller makes the argument that the point of all this talk of mystery and revelation is not to solve the mystery; the point of interrogating the mystery is to gain *resolution* or what she calls "the resolute."[230]

> "Becoming what you never dared" takes resolve. [The resolute] . . . appeared in each case differently: as relationality itself, as testimony, as the *creation ex profundis*, as the omni-amorous power, as the lure that dares us, as the agapic justice, as the basileic process. And in each case, as in a parable, the sense of resolve does not solve but deepens the mystery.[231]

Deepening the mystery is exactly what I hope for with *missio Dei*. Is *missio Dei* imperfect because it cannot solve the mystery that defines (or fails to define) Christian mission? Absolutely. But I do not see that as grounds for dismissing it as no longer useful. Any theologizing on the nature of the divine is bound to be fallible because humans are fallible, and we are the ones who theologize. So, searching for the perfectly universal and definitive concept of mission in the twenty-first century (or any other century, for that matter) is futile. Rather than dismiss the concept of *missio Deo* for its failings, instead I argue that we commit to a more holistic and engaged interrogation of it. Not to solve the mystery—but to deepen it. Next, we must dive deeper into the work of exploring the mystery of Christian mission from an explicitly Indigenous perspective.

Four

Beyond Enemy Lines and Towards Re-Integration

IN THIS CHAPTER I will build a foundation for writing constructive missiology from an Indigenous perspective. This hopeful work of integrating an Indigenist perspective into missiology happens behind enemy lines. I say this because to be an Indigenous person in a dominantly non-Indigenous society is to live behind enemy lines. To write theology as an Indigenous person using epistemological arguments from non-theological disciplines to critique hegemonic Western theological perspectives is to work from behind enemy lines. In chapter two I outlined some decolonized Indigenous epistemologies. In this chapter I continue to work across disciplines as I present three necessary principles for developing an Indigenous missiology. To arrive at an Indigenous missiology is to move past living and working *behind* enemy lines and get to a place *beyond* enemy lines.

The first principle is that an Indigenous approach to missiology needs to be from the perspective of the oppressed, the marginalized, or the underside.[232] While traditional ecumenical writings on mission have tended to be inclusive in terms of global perspective, almost without exception the experiences of those being ministered to in the name of mission are mentioned only in service of the dominant in the missionary relationship. The stories of those made marginal are shared in service of those with power when it suits their narratives. If we want to decentre the dominant perspective and re-write the story of missions from the point of view of the colonized and the oppressed, then we must give their stories and perspectives primacy. The most recent statement on mission from the World Council of Churches Commission on World Mission and Evangelism, "Together Towards Life: Mission and Evangelism in Changing Landscapes,"[233] purports to be written from the margins, but in my view, it *incorporates* perspectives of those who have been made marginal without *privileging* them. The document explains mission's complicity with colonialism and oppression, and says that mission needs to shift from being "mission *to* the margins" to being "mission *from* the margins" and defines how people are marginalized, but then doesn't dig into how mission would be reshaped if that were so.

The second principle is that, in keeping with common characteristics of Indigenous epistemologies, an Indigenous approach to mission must be political, ethical, pedagogical, or some combination of the three. As I have written elsewhere,[234] Indigenous oral traditions are not about simply recounting stories without intent and discernment. Indigenous orality was a method for considering the interaction of different facets of life: physical, contextual, relational, emotional, pedagogical, ethical, historical. Once the teller of a story viewed a situation from a particular perspective, they would then recount a story that responded to that situation politically, ethically, or pedagogically. The storyteller would make nuanced changes in perspective depending on the perceived needs of the hearer. Likewise, an Indigenous approach to mission grounded in Indigenous epistemologies will attempt to respond politically, ethically, and pedagogically while at the same time attempting to avoid binary dualisms and exclusivity. This approach is good news to Indigenous communities and reflects the evangelical nature of missiology.

The third principle is that an Indigenous method for approaching missiology will not only need to be interdisciplinary—to speak intelligently from epistemological, political, sociological, pedagogical, and ethical perspectives—but must also be intercultural. Intercultural theology insists that we not only agree to come together from multiple cultural backgrounds, but that we commit to being transformed by the perspective of the other, without smoothing multiple perspectives into a singular narrative. An intercultural theological approach to mission for Indigenous people must speak to the continued impact of hegemonic theological perspectives. It must explicitly or implicitly ask those who are invested in the hegemonic position to be changed by Indigenous realities and views. This work will only be successful if the decentring and disruption of theology from Indigenous undersides starts to transform dominant societies.

I will spend the rest of this chapter expanding on these three principles.

Principle One: Views from the Underside of Colonization[235]

In his book *Against War: Views from the Underside of Modernity*, Nelson Maldonado-Torres traces the epistemological primacy of colonization to the year 1492, which, in his view, is a crucial point for understanding European society's development of a "paradigm of war."[236] I believe that North American society has also developed a parallel paradigm of colonization. In his book *The Idea of Latin America*, Walter Mignolo argues that:

> Christian cosmology . . . organized the world into continents revolving around Europe. The fact that those in Cuzco or Tenochtitlan, capitals of the Inca and Aztec Empires, conceived of themselves as living in the center of space would have no bearing on the maps that were drawn [by Europeans].[237]

Over the past half a millennium the centring of European civilization has persisted socially, politically, and theologically as well. Nevertheless, important work is being done in Indigenous communities, national churches, and international Christian bodies to reverse this Eurocentricity. Indigenous communities are developing theologies that are consistent with historical Christian theology but disrupt Eurocentric understandings of faithfulness in liberative ways. I believe that without the possibilities presented by these theologies, there cannot be a faith that is worth following.

The late missionary Vincent Donovan argued that the message of Christianity is one that can be accepted or rejected.[238] Donovan wrote "that somewhere close to the heart of Christianity lies the terrible and mysterious possibility of rejection; that no Christianity has any meaning or value, if there is not freedom to accept it or reject it."[239] This is a simple but profound concept, and it is crucially important because an inclusive faith must not only be ontologically open to the possibility of rejection, it must also communicate that possibility in the way it is practised or embodied. Within missiological literature very few theologians and practitioners make this important claim, but I believe it is crucial to the promotion of an epistemologically inclusive faith.

Historically, the church has attached much of its value to its missionary work, both local and overseas. That work has had specific objectives, such as increasing revenues, memberships, or conversions, or simple "charity" based on a concept of developing those who are "less than." But when the church invests too much of its purpose in those outcomes, then it fails to offer a meaningful choice; there is only one right answer.

Mignolo's observations in *The Idea of Latin America* are mostly political and historical, but they have theological implications as well. In his history of Europe centring itself as the privileged society against which all others were measured, he includes the role that theology played: "Theology provided the authority of the locus of observation and cartography the truth of the world being observed."[240] As Europe conquered the world, it classified the world being conquered.[241] This centring took hold in politics, economics, art, and literature.

Understanding how Europe became the zero-point of observation of the rest of the world is critical to a theological undertaking that seeks to uproot dominant perspectives. While the interdisciplinary efforts in postcolonial studies are important, and there are parallels in those colonized histories to Indigenous experiences, Indigenous approaches to theology in the Americas cannot simply seek to move past colonization.

The fact that "the West" includes the Americas (over against Africa and "the East") is evidence of the *fait accompli* nature of colonization in the Americas. While Canada and the United States of America rank among the world's top eight economies, the other countries of the Americas (divided along economic lines of north and south) still manage to be on the "right side" of the (cultural) spectrum in historically Eurocentric terms. These other countries, especially the richer countries of the southern Americas, are ranked as less than the economic superpowers only because of their less developed economies and their cultural ties to Spain and Portugal rather than England (the most recent and biggest winner in the European drive to colonize the rest of the world). If forced to cast the net of the West wider, they would be included as a natural extended family of North America and Europe in the classification of the "other" who threatens the global privilege of the West.

While colonization is more complete in some countries than others, the fact that the most dominant tiers of society tend to come from European heritage is evidence that Europe was on the winning side of colonization in the Americas. There is no "post-colonial" context here. Rather, any theological effort to uproot European epistemological hegemonies must be seen as inherently anti-colonial. Anti-colonial Indigenous intellectual projects may involve physically removing colonial presences or privileging perspectives from an Indigenous territory or conquered land. For my purposes here, I refer to anti-colonialism as the intent to disrupt European epistemologies that created systems that privilege those of European descent and oppress Indigenous communities and newer classes of migrants.

Principle Two: Political, Ethical, Pedagogical

If an Indigenous approach to mission is to be political, ethical, pedagogical, or some combination of the three, then it must face the lived realities of human bodies. I argued in chapter two that Indigenous approaches to liberation must include a pedagogical dimension. I believe that they must teach a political re-reading of the relationship between Indigenous and Settler/Arrivant societies. Gutiérrez reminds us in the introduction to *Las Casas: In Search of the Poor of Jesus Christ*[242] that facing the truth is important because the very act of facing the truth is part of what liberates us from the history that Settler/Arrivant and Indigenous societies share in America.[243]

In this chapter I do not try to lift up pre-Christian or non-Christian Indigenous traditions that are marginalized in the academy or that have clashed with Christianity in the past. For this reason, there may be some in Indigenous communities who consider *me* the enemy, as a Christian theologian. Yet, as an Indigenous woman, theologian, scholar, poet, and ordained minister, I find myself behind enemy lines on a regular basis; simply raising my voice is an act of resistance. And I believe my voice is an important one at a time when marginalized voices throughout the academy are calling for a reclamation of liberation thought.

I grew up in the shadow of a formidable woman. My mother was and is a passionate, outspoken, theologically prophetic woman who challenged the churches to take seriously the concerns and struggles resulting from oppression of Indigenous Peoples in *Kanata* and around the world. Although my mother had no formal theological training, I grew up hearing names like Gutiérrez, Freire, Daly, and Reuther on her lips and the lips of her colleagues in their struggle for self-determination. As a six-year-old, I could not have defined liberation theology, but I knew it existed, and I knew it was important.

Fast forward to my own theological formation. As a seminarian in a mainstream mainline Protestant theological institution, I was often asked by professors and church leaders—leaders from Settler society who had once been inspired by the radical propositions of Gutiérrez and the other liberationists—why liberation theology hadn't worked in North America as it had in Latin America. The questions carried an undertone of resigned lament. At the time, I assumed, in my own naïve way, that the answer was due to demographic differences: in Latin America and in South Africa the oppressed were a majority of the population, whereas in North America they were a minority. But after years of reading the foundational writings of liberationists and doing my own scholarly research, I came to see this demographic difference as less important than I had thought. My answer to this question now is that liberation theology has not taken root in North America, beyond a few congregations or pockets of community organizing, because of a failure to understand the difference between method and process. The route to liberation is a *process* of conscientization. Instead, it has been applied as a simple band-aid over the festering wounds of oppression on this half of the continent. Even when church leaders are profoundly influenced on a personal intellectual level by liberation theology, they consistently apply it as a model rather than experience it as a process, as articulated by Gutiérrez, Freire, and others.

One Indigenous thinker who has undergone his own process of conscientization is *Ts'msyen* lawyer Calvin Helin. In his controversial book *Dances with Dependency: Indigenous Success through Self-Reliance,* he identified the "lateral violence" that exists in Indigenous communities whereby successive generations of Native peoples reenact and perpetuate systems of violence against each other, as an alternative to engaging in acts of violence against the state.[244] As previously noted, this dynamic is like the one Cornel West names as the nihilism experienced by Black men in America because of systemic oppression.[245]

In response, Helin called for First Nations in *Kanata* to resist continued dependence on the state because the state would not upset the status quo by doing anything to resolve native claims for justice in any sphere of life. I agree with the stated outcome. As time has progressed, it's become evident that Helin wants us to get our piece of the "status quo" economic pie, not that he wants us to claim authentically Indigenous ways to do business differently.

Helin writes for a general audience rather than an academic one. He brands his ideas as "Nike" actions: Overcome poverty by "just doing it." He draws on mainstream Canadian newspapers for most of his source material, which leaves his work open to academic criticism, but he remains strongly grounded in *Ts'msyen* culture. He sees his leadership role as consistent with the chieftainships in his family, and he traces his ideas back to the teachings of his father and grandmothers. This makes him an important thinker in very traditional and very practical ways. Fiscally and politically more conservative than most Indigenous leadership in my own circles, he is forging his own path to overcoming centuries of oppression in the ways he knows how. Indigenous Voices are not homogeneous, and although I would seek different methods for liberation from the dependency relationship between Indigenous Peoples in *Kanata* and the state, our goals are the same.

Helin's economic critique and Gutiérrez's theological one complement each other. Both want to move communities of the oppressed from states of oppression and dependence to development and liberation. Together they bring liberation back to the table of theological discourse, but as a process of conscientization rather than as a model of theological education. I want to take a closer look here at some of the principles underpinning Gutiérrez's liberation theology.

First, liberation theology, like the development theories of the past forty years, will go nowhere without a commitment to actively critique evil as it manifests itself in individual action and systemic oppression. Competition for development dollars will not lead oppressed communities into liberation, only into an internal replication of the unjust socio-economic structures under which they find themselves pinned.

Second, liberation theology must challenge the epistemological hegemony of Western scholarship based on the thinking of Descartes, Kant, and Hegel. This hegemony of thought shaped biblical exegesis and theological proposals up until the past half century. Gutiérrez critiques these philosophers' views of the world as both destructive and self-centred. Instead of the traditional European notion that concepts ought not to conform to objects, an alternative view holds that objects in the world should conform to our conceptions. If we fail to challenge these epistemological strongholds, the only outcome we will be able to offer Indigenous people is assimilation or a capitalist form of success that doesn't challenge the socio-economic status quo. Unseating a Western epistemology does not mean returning to an anachronistic reclaiming of truly "tribal" practices[246]—a notion fiercely challenged by many Indigenous scholars, including Māori theologian Jenny Plane Te Paa—but rather articulating an epistemology that transcends a romanticized historical view and interrupts the current cycle of oppression and violence faced by Indigenous and other marginalized groups. As Gutiérrez writes in *Las Casas*:

> A consideration of what happened from the sixteenth century onward must not be transformed into an invitation to turn back the clock of history. History cannot be remade. This is simple realism. But this must not prevent us—on the contrary, it should stimulate us—to see

> the meaning for us today of an honest interpretation of the events that have occurred since that time.[247]

Third, we must allow marginalized and traumatized people to voice their own perspectives on the past and the present. Gutiérrez uses Freud's revolutionized personal psychology to highlight the need for individual transformation to accompany mass social transformation, but Freudian psychology may not be the most appropriate methodology for treating Indigenous survivors of perpetual colonization. Indigenous survivors suffer from individual and generational post-traumatic stress disorders which Western psychologies tend to pathologize as an inability to "get over" the abuses experienced under colonization. "If we are to talk of revolution today our talk will be meaningless unless we effect some union between the macro-social and micro-social, and between 'inner reality' and 'outer reality,'" Gutiérrez writes.[248] Here is a point of intersection between Gutiérrez and Helin. In the very first paragraphs of his chapter on transformation from grievance to development, Helin argues for a process of psychological transformation in the individual: "The basic purpose of grieving is to allow for a period of adjustment to a psychological trauma."[249] Allowing marginalized and traumatized voices to raise alternative perspectives on the past and the present is a political as well as a pedagogical act.

In the first chapter of her book *Indecent Theology: Theological Perversions in Sex, Gender and Politics*, Argentinian liberation theologian Marcella Althaus-Reid recounted the demise of pre-colonial Latin American Grand Narratives. "Cultural, religious, socio-political discourses, economy and science, and philosophical cosmovisions which defined identity, meaning and patterns of social organization and sexual constructions were obliterated from the earth."[250] She described the specific concurrent traumas of literal and figurative silencing of Indigenous Peoples: "'Tongues' were lost; mother tongues were buried while human tongues were cut from mouths. Women's tongues were silenced for centuries. What survived entered into a covenant of silence, and since then it has never fully spoken again."[251] In her novel *Daughters Are Forever*, the late *Stó:lō* novelist Lee Maracle described that history as "500 years of 'hush, don't cry.'"[252] Indigenous people have been forced to respect this coercion to silence instead of screaming in terror and frustration. It will be important for both Indigenous and Settler communities to make space for the healing of individuals and communities as part of the transformative process. This will involve raising political and pedagogical voices to reframe the dominant historical and contemporary narratives of colonization, racism, and land and resource rights. For liberation to begin, the dominant in society will have to find the moral will and love to resist the urge to force Indigenous voices, now raised in pain and anger, back into silence.

The fourth and final principle underlying Gutiérrez's liberation theology I want to highlight is related to the first: A commitment to confronting evil means that those who perpetuate systems of injustice must be held accountable. The nihilism, indifference, lateral wounding, and corruption in Indigenous communities make it easy for Settler societies to fall back on racist and genocidal justifications to absolve themselves of any personal guilt for a historical process that started five hundred years ago. This is where the real work for Settler communities begins. "Only by looking at the historical truth full in the face shall we be able to embark upon the times to come with responsibility and efficacy," Gutiérrez writes.[253] Later he adds: "Those who had not seen the abuse and contempt to which the Indians were subjected, those who had not suffered in their own flesh the aggression of the mighty ones of the Indies, those who had not counted dead bodies, had other priorities in theology."[254] Things are not so different now; those who have not counted the bodies have other priorities. It is easy to avoid becoming accountable for the dispossession and dehumanizing of Indigenous and other marginalized communities.

Here is where we return to the concept of *missio Dei* and the failure of this theological construct to act alongside liberation theology to work towards transformation and liberation for Indigenous Peoples. *Missio Dei* was supposed to liberate missiology from its ties to colonialism by shifting the focus of mission from the actions of individuals and churches to the ontological mission of God, one that presupposes a divine desire for life for all in abundance. This sounds good in theory. But when the discourse is dominated by theologians trained in European and American theological schools who, regardless of how liberal they are, have an almost unchallenged possessive investment in their Whiteness, we can understand that there might be some problems in the execution of such a transformation.

Not surprisingly, there have been challenges to *missio Dei* from both African and Asian regions to ensure that the lived realities of the people are the context in which *missio Dei* is grounded, because God's kingdom intends that each being should have life and have it in abundance. These challenges are echoed in Latin American thought as well as Indigenous theologies (although Indigenous theology challenges the anthropocentric idea of human beings as the starting point for reconciliation). These critiques bring us back to the concept of God's preferential option for the poor.

Any postcolonial theology of mission must take seriously the concerns raised by voices at the margins: women, Indigenous Peoples, the poor, the Global South, and anyone else who is othered by the hegemonic drives of the Western academy and by dominant church structures. As Elisabeth Schüssler Fiorenza points out:

> Since no foolproof recipe for how to go about producing a feminist reading is available, feminist interpreters do not subscribe to one single reading strategy and interpretive method . . . Hence, I suggest that feminist interpretive methods are best understood as ways of engaging in the process and movement of conscientization.[255]

I argue the same is true for postcolonial and Indigenous approaches to missiology. This is why, in support of Helin's desire to lift up Indigenous communities, I want to join the chorus of scholars who are seeking to reclaim liberation theology for the twenty-first century.[256] There are no foolproof recipes, but rather our focus should be on processes of conscientization, however they are appropriate and however they develop in myriad and organic ways.

Principle Three: Intercultural Perspectives on Liberation and Theology

I first became aware of the distinction between the terms "multicultural," "cross-cultural," and "intercultural" in 2006 when The United Church of Canada took an action at the meeting of its 39th General Council to create resources to help the denomination develop into an intentionally intercultural church. In a multicultural society, according to the United Church, "we value tolerance, and celebrate one another's culturally distinctive cuisine, dress, music, dance, and related outward expressions of culture. It usually requires only superficial and polite social interaction."[257] Cross-cultural communities take a step further along from mere tolerance and diversity towards relationality: "We try to build bridges of relationship between our cultural communities by sharing, listening, learning, and being open to changing. It usually requires intentionality, and programs of education and community-building."[258]

Interculturalism, however, offers an altogether different approach to living together as separate and distinct cultures who impact and intentionally transform each other. The United Church defines it this way:

> Our social structures and everyday interactions are defined by justice, mutuality, respect, equality, understanding, acceptance, freedom, diversity, peace-making, and celebration. Intercultural community hopes to take us deeper than multicultural or cross-cultural models of community.[259]

A defining characteristic of interculturalism, as understood by those leading the process, is the necessity of addressing racial and economic power imbalances.[260]

The most well-intentioned non-Indigenous people in North American society vastly underestimate both the scale of the task of addressing racial and economic power imbalances and the positive impact it could have. It is much easier to point fingers at others who say or do things that are clearly more racist than anything we would say or do. It only takes searching for an article relating to Indigenous issues in Canada (or the United States) to see the back and forth fighting over bigotry and the attempt to not appear bigoted by non-Indigenous Peoples in the dominant society. For example, in an online article of *The Globe and Mail* (a national print and online newspaper with a readership that spans the country) entitled "Ottawa to spend $1.2-billion on hospital for First Nations in Northern Ontario, after weeks of pressure,"[261] there is the perception (either overtly or covertly) that the positive impact of this funding on an Indigenous community would either a) result in a negative impact on non-Indigenous people across the country, or b) is undeserved and any complaints about inequality are no different than other inequalities suffered by other strata of society and therefore Indigenous aid should not be given in any preferential way. For example, one reader comments:

> 2.7 billion to serve 12,000 people. Something to remember next time you read an article about FN's not getting their "fair share." Apply the same $225,000 per capita cost to Vancouver area with 3,000,000 people and you get $775,000,000,000!!! I know it will cost a lot more to build something in the North, but this is almost beyond comprehension.[262]

Even more overtly resistant were the following two comments: "The other issue is using taxpayer dollars to pay for something that people who don't pay taxes will use. Maybe if they want a fancy new hospital they can cough up some cash also? We've surely given them enough over the years,"[263] and: "Nice to see the Federal Government step up to the plate but it will never be enough for our First Nation friends. No one is ever satisfied and grateful has an expiry clock!"[264]

Comments such as these are, sadly, common. They reveal the brokenness of society—both for Settler/Arrivant and Indigenous communities. While it can be tempting to dismiss comments such as these as individual opinions unrepresentative of Indigenous-Settler relations in *Kanata*, people who hold these views are precisely the people the church could be educating and nudging down a different path. We must not forget that these views persist in the church. However, such individual opinions are not the biggest challenge to becoming an intercultural society.

The real work is to identify and dismantle the structures in society that perpetuate inequality and that are widely supported, even by people who don't think they are racist. For example, let us consider the contemporary treaty negotiation process in British Columbia. To believe that this treaty negotiation process will finally and fairly deal with the issue of unceded traditional territories is to ignore the vast power imbalance that exists in the relationship from the outset. While the public may hear that a treaty negotiation is based on nation-to-nation relationships between Canada and a given First Nation, the Canadian government has already set parameters around what is and is not up for negotiation. *Kanien'kehaka* scholar Taiaiake Alfred deconstructs the problem:

> This [problem] is clearly evident in the province's "Principles for Negotiating Treaties":
>
> - Private property is not on the table.
> - Jurisdictional certainty between First Nations and municipalities must be clearly spelled out.
> - Continued access to hunting, fishing and recreational opportunities will be guaranteed.
> - The Canadian Constitution and Charter of Rights and Freedoms will continue to apply equally to all British Columbians.
> - Agreements must be affordable to all British Columbians.
> - The federal government's primary constitutional and financial responsibility for treaties must be maintained.
> - Fair compensation for unavoidable disruption of commercial interests will be assured.
> - Province-wide standards of resource management and environmental protection will continue to apply.[265]

This is how colonial governments exert power over Indigenous claimants, by defining in advance how the relationship will be transformed. But governments do not stop there. In the interest of "fairness" they also privilege Settler interests in other ways:

> To further limit the parameters of treaty negotiations, both federal and provincial governments have instituted "advisory councils" of

> non-Indigenous people and commercial interests. Thus on top of the limitations imposed by the basic positions outlined above, the federal and provincial governments work with the Settlers and organized commercial interests who currently occupy and use the lands under negotiation to develop the mandates their negotiators use to deal with Indigenous people.[266]

So, negotiations are not between equal powers, each with sovereignty and self-determination, and the rules are not fair because the party with the power defines the parameters of the negotiation. Meanwhile, the party with the power solicits and prioritizes the interests of the Settler society while the interests of the Indigenous communities are assumed to be fully and completely represented by whichever group sits at the negotiating table, with little concern given to difference of politics, corruption, or diversity of opinion in the Indigenous communities.

The work of moving towards interculturalism involves naming these power imbalances and deconstructing layers of racial, economic, and political privileges. But at the root of all these privileges lies an epistemological privilege that must also be challenged. For Settlers to be open to transformation, they must first believe that Indigenous Peoples have something to teach.

Viola Cordova, the first Native American woman to receive a PhD in philosophy, spoke about the resistance she faced in placing her Native-grounded scholarly arguments on equal footing with traditional Western philosophical traditions. She named Indigenous worldviews as mainstream because they are the result of centuries of "analyzing the world and our place in it."[267] Yet she cautioned her students against unbridled enthusiasm for pursuing an academic course of study that attempted to validate Indigenous perspectives:

> If your intention is to translate Kant or Descartes into your own Native language or to give up your own views for those of the dominant culture, then the university will applaud and assist you. If, however, your intention is, as mine has been, to seek a method by which your own views can be articulated and examined, then you should be prepared for comments like these:

> "You must not make the mistake of attributing sophisticated notions to primitive minds."
>
> "The notions, if they are there, are not intentional."
>
> "Native American art is not a subject for an aesthetics course; the style is, as are all primitive styles, automatic (i.e. unintentional)."
>
> "The Greeks were not a primitive people!" (On my attempt to trace the similarities in Greek drama and Native American rituals.)
>
> In other words, the Native American is not seen as a valid thinker. He is, at most, a living fossil through which Euroman can trace his own rise to his present stage of achievement.[268]

Without such challenges to Western epistemological privilege, I don't believe it will be possible for Christianity to open itself to transformation by simply adapting its narratives and praxis to the perspective of Indigenous cultures. We must raise voices that offer a different and insistent Indigenous narrative to transform the understanding of Settlers. In this, I am attempting to set the stage for a new relationship altogether. From that new relationship, perhaps the church can be transformed as well as be transforming.

Anthropologist Julie Cruikshank identifies a tendency in academic circles to dismiss the importance of individual and collective stories of lives lived. She writes:

> the lesson I learned . . . is that narratives providing the most helpful guidance are inevitably locally grounded, highly particular, and culturally specific. What is important is not just knowing the story, but sharing the context for knowing when and why it is told so that conversations can build on that shared knowledge.[269]

My hope is that by allowing politically marginalized voices to guide intercultural conversations, Settler societies will come to a deeper understanding of oppression and genocide. We are not a broken record. Each time a memory is evoked a context is being raised. Each time a story is told there is a purpose to the story's telling, an invitation to listen. These are the bases upon which a constructive Indigenous theology of mission needs to be written. An Indigenous theology of mission must be firmly rooted in a commitment to interculturalism and to the political concerns of marginalized Indigenous communities. A commitment to solidary, justice, and liberation is essential to the theological process. In the final chapter of this book, I will begin that constructive theological task.

Five

Constructing Indigenous Missiology

I thank my God every time I remember you, constantly praying with joy in every one of my prayers for all of you, because of your sharing in the gospel from the first day until now. I am confident of this, that the one who began a good work among you will bring it to completion by the day of Jesus Christ. It is right for me to think this way about all of you, because you hold me in your heart, for all of you share in God's grace with me, both in my imprisonment and in the defence and confirmation of the gospel. For God is my witness, how I long for all of you with the compassion of Christ Jesus. And this is my prayer, that your love may overflow more and more with knowledge and full insight to help you to determine what is best, so that on the day of Christ you may be pure and blameless, having produced the harvest of righteousness that comes through Jesus Christ for the glory and praise of God.

—*Philippians 1.3–11*

Those who know suffering come closer to the truth about creation: the future is open, alarmingly or promisingly. The way is not laid out in advance. Creation itself is in process. Our own way forward has not yet been charted. There may be no trail before us at all. Sometimes one can only move forward in faith: that is, in courage and confidence, not in a delusional certainty.

—*Catherine Keller,* On the Mystery

IN CHAPTER THREE I made an argument for mission as solidarity, mission as the quest for justice, mission as liberation, and mission as theology. In this chapter I will attempt to develop three of these themes, further considering the issues I raised earlier: power analysis, race relations, and finance. I will leave the theme of mission as theology for my conclusion. Since all the perspectives in my theologies of mission offered here are undergirded by a commitment to intercultural theology,[270] let me further explore the topic of interculturalism.

Intercultural Theology as a Basis

In 2006, when the United Church made a commitment to becoming an intentionally intercultural church, they developed a definition of "intercultural" as a commitment to deeper engagement and mutual transformation between peoples and cultural groups. "It means living together with a respectful awareness of each other's differences. We do this by examining ourselves, building relationships, and distributing power fairly."[271] Intercultural is not a substitute for "ethnic"; it is about mutually reciprocal relationships among and between cultural groups who learn and grow together. The focus of intercultural ministry is relationship building, deep connections, mutual gifting, and learning from one another.

These points sum up my own approach to interculturalism, as both a scholar and a member of the United Church of Canada. This approach is not simply an argument against inculturation or acculturation,[272] both of which seem too anthropologically focused, but rather an approach to contextuality, to being open to transforming and being transformed by others. This is not to say that all contextual theologies are intercultural, but rather that contextual theologies open the door to liberation, revelation, and transformation—if the individuals or groups are open to the potential of mutual transformation.

I believe this approach to interculturalism helps to build intimate communities where racial, socio-economic, and cultural power imbalances are identified and addressed. Intercultural practice, to me, becomes the closest means of analysing culture and Christian theology as a Freirean means of liberation of both Indigenous and Settler communities. While Freire's focus was on education and pedagogical models, he outlined a liberatory practice he called "co-intentional education." This practice was based on his understanding that "[t]eachers and students (leadership and people), co-intent on reality, are both Subjects, not only in the task of unveiling that reality, and thereby coming to know it critically, but in the task of re-creating that knowledge."[273]

For Indigenous epistemologies to liberate missiology from Eurocentric assumptions, both Indigenous and Settler communities must be committed to a critical evaluation of their contexts and must be, as Freire puts it, co-intent on re-creating reality. This contrasts with the views of Volker Küster who, despite his intention to confront Eurocentrism, remains focused on the transformation of the marginalized (read, in his case: migrant) communities. Küster, a pioneer of intercultural theology in European academic theology, argues for "integration" over assimilation. But read from the perspective of Indigenous or marginalized peoples, his distinction is not as stark as he would have hoped. Küster defines integration this way:

> Integration in a positive sense means that migrants should participate in the receiving culture without neglecting their own cultural and religious identity. Being bilingual, accepting the norms of the common justice system, and accepting pluralism are important benchmarks. Commitment to integration leads to tension between the "universal equality" of persons as individuals (as that is condensed in discussions that centre on human dignity and human rights) and the politics of recognition and difference (which implies that persons belong to or are embedded within certain groups).[274]

According to the liberationist models put forward by Gutiérrez, Freire, and others, both the receiving communities and the migrant communities should be transformed. What Küster proposes instead is that the migrant communities essentially assimilate without abandoning their own cultural roots and practices.

I join The United Church of Canada in arguing for a commitment to examining the socio-economic and cultural roots of systems of oppression and marginalization so that both dominant and marginalized can seek liberation and transformation as part of the praxis of Christian mission. In the context of Christian communities, this would be a co-intentional liberatory move towards both *metanoia* (change or conversion) and *koinonia* (joint contribution).

This is not easy work, by any means. Reinhold Niebuhr wrote about the interactions between dominant societies and those on the underside in *Moral Man and Immoral Society*. While this is a dated source, its description of the self-justification of social privilege remains helpful:

> it is always possible for social privilege to justify itself, at least in its own eyes, in terms of the social function which it renders. If the argument is to be plausible, when used by privileged classes who possess hereditary advantages, it must be proved or assumed that the underprivileged classes would not have the capacity of rendering the same service if given the same opportunity. This assumption is invariably made by the privileged classes . . . It has always been the habit of privileged groups to deny the oppressed classes every opportunity for the cultivation of innate capacities and then to accuse them of lacking what they have been denied the right to acquire.[275]

It is precisely because of this power dynamic that, I argue, there are two main tracks that missiology must pursue. The first track is missiology as it applies to Indigenous communities and other communities from the margins, and the second and more important track is missiology for the dominant in society. While God is calling each of us to walk in faithful discipleship, what that discipleship looks like is radically different for different communities.

While I am establishing a binary here that is undoubtedly problematic, I am drawing a distinction, not along racial or ethnic lines, but between oppressed and oppressor. I mentioned in chapter three, that, as with feminist biblical interpretation, there is no foolproof method for developing an Indigenist or postcolonial theology; what remains important is the process of conscientization. In other words, the experiences that shed light on and help in the process of conscientization come from all aspects of life for both Indigenous Peoples and Settlers and are all important in the shared journey of solidarity.

Mission as Solidarity: A View Towards Interdependence

> In my great grandfather's time, the people traveled the NorthWest coast by large hand-hewn cedar canoes, marriages were arranged, and Chiefs strategically built their wealth. Has the present made us relics of the past, a conquered and defeated people with a history irrelevant to today's society? Is assimilation into the society of the "civilized" the only rational decision? No, this conclusion cannot and must not be accepted, for if we—we being both the colonizer and the colonized—succumb to such a strategy, we lose principles and perspectives that have the ability to transform the emptiness of nothingness to balance. The war we find ourselves thrust into blindfolded is not against human beings, although human beings and human systems must be held accountable for the wrongdoings of the past and present. Our struggle is against the human weavings of injustice, discrimination and violence creating a robe signifying supremacy of the colonizer over the colonized. The self-proclamation of superiority founded on the notion of progress is the robe that conceals a known and unknown (unknown because the deceased cannot voice their experience) vast number of crimes against Indigenous Peoples of North America.
>
> —*Patricia June Vickers*[276]

Given the brokenness in both Indigenous cultures and traditional Western missiology, we need to construct a healthy, interdependent theology of mission with others, or mission as solidarity, that honours the traditional teachings of Indigenous Peoples. This is important to our people who still identify, however tenuously, as Christian, but it is also important for the stretching of global Christianity if it is to grow, evolve, and change. The kingdom of God requires the established order—which some call "empire"—to be changed by those who are now on the margins.

This is a risky venture. But risk is what we are being called to. In 2009, I visited a *Haíłzaqv* woman in the hospital in my mother's home village. She was newly sober, as was her husband. She had four children, aged three to twenty-one, and a four-month-old grandson. She had stage three Hodgkin type B lymphoma. I asked her if she was receiving the support she needed from her family. She proceeded to describe the difficult life situations of each member of her family and her husband's family. Then she said that she didn't ask for help. I reflected out loud that it sounded as if it was easier for her to face her disease alone and lonely than to risk being hurt by family members who were unwilling or unable to be there to support her. She started to cry.

I wonder if sometimes our theologies shy away from interdependence and intimate interculturalism for this same reason. We are afraid of being let down. I have shared the ways in which the church has broken my heart, an experience shared by a multitude of others. The risky, intimate, and messy work of conscientization that I am recommending is perhaps *too* scandalous and fraught with peril for Settler/Arrivant communities.

Indigenous philosophies and epistemologies consistently challenge the individualism of Western culture. Meanwhile, our cultures are examined, studied, classified, and objectified, but their teachings are not integrated into the wider search for the abundant life that we believe, as Christians, God wills for humanity. Viola Cordova wrote about this dynamic:

> Today the field of Native American philosophy is dominated by non-Native Americans. One reason is the small number of Native Americans trained in philosophical methodologies, but another reason is that often the Native American is seen as too *subjective*, too immersed in his own culture, to participate in an *objective* examination. On the other hand, the Native American trained in philosophical methodologies is excluded from dealing with topics that are "Western"

> on the basis that since he comes from outside the culture, he cannot truly understand the full scope of Western thought.[277]

She names the inherent contradiction in the system: "In the one case 'subjectivity' is a flaw, in the other, a requirement!"[278] In this way, Indigenous scholars are blocked from making any progress towards changing the dominant worldview of Western empiricism. Indigenous theorist Linda Tuhiwai Smith acknowledges the tension experienced by Indigenous intellectuals who achieve, by way of their education, a privileged status within Indigenous communities: "Despite the very powerful issues which locate many First World indigenous peoples in Third World social conditions we still, comparatively speaking, occupy a place of privilege within the world of indigenous peoples."[279] She goes on to explain the dynamic already articulated by Cordova:

> One of the many criticisms that gets leveled at indigenous intellectuals or activists is that our Western education precludes us from writing or speaking from a "real" and authentic indigenous position. Of course, those who do speak from a more "traditional" indigenous point of view are criticized because they do not make sense ("speak English, what!"). Or, our talk is reduced to some "nativist" discourse, dismissed by colleagues in the academy as naïve, contradictory and illogical.[280]

This contributes to the invisibility of Indigenous scholars and Indigenous intellectualism, making it that much harder for Indigenous people to assert their political and legal rights.

The Western—and particularly North American—denial around the rights of Indigenous Peoples in *Kanata* and the US is virulent. For example, Tom Flanagan, in an opinion piece on reparations and reconciliation, writes:

> Payment of reparations to historically mistreated racial minorities, especially people of African origin, is a lively topic of discussion in the United States and other countries where slavery was institutionalized. In Canada, reparations have been paid to First Nations for almost two decades under the somewhat misleading heading of Reconciliation. The expansion of reparations has been driven by developments in

> the judicial process, especially the use of class-action lawsuits and the instructions for Justice Canada to negotiate rather than litigate. And, aside from the large sums paid out in compensation, there are two serious political consequences: elected representatives have no meaningful oversight of the negotiations and, contrary to Canadian legal tradition, individual claims of mistreatment are not merely leading to compensation but are being used to overturn core government policies enacted by previous Parliaments.[281]

It is much more difficult to find such overt opinions in North American theological writing, because for the most part Indigenous concerns are simply not discussed in theology.

In much theological discourse, the "oppressed" refers to people in the Global South, people in Guatemala or Colombia or the Philippines, kids on television in charity ads with swollen bellies and flies on their faces. It seldom includes American Indians or Canadian First Nations, Inuit, or Métis.

For example, in October 2008 I had the opportunity to participate in a World Council of Churches' program for just and inclusive communities in Baguio City, the Philippines. During one conversation, an Indigenous layperson from the Philippines accused both a Sámi theologian and me of not understanding Indigenous contexts of poverty because we were from democratic socialist countries that provide free housing to Indigenous Peoples. My Sámi colleague was quick to respond: "Yes, but only because our colonizers have impeded or completely prevented our ability to live in traditional ways, and if they didn't provide housing to us in sub-zero temperatures, we would die!"

What would true interdependence between Indigenous populations of North America and its dominant Settler societies look like? It would require a vast re-visioning of the political situation. It is no surprise, then, that Indigenous theologians are calling for a contextual Indigenous theology that is inherently political in nature.[282]

There is also the relativity of poverty and freedom. Nobel laureate economist Amartya Sen writes about the dynamic of being poor in North America as opposed to the Global South. Many of the statistics relating to the

Canadian Indigenous context were outlined in chapter one. Both in Canada and the United States there is a racialization of poverty where Indigenous Peoples (followed by other marginalized people of colour, especially African Americans) have higher rates of poverty and lower life expectancies than their White compatriots.

In exploring this racialization of American poverty (both Canadian and in the United States), Sen writes:

> Indeed, in a comparison with the population of third world counties, African Americans may well be a great many times richer in terms of incomes, even after taking note of price differences. Seen this way, the deprivation of the American blacks seems to pale to insignificance in the international perspective.
>
> But is income the right space in which to make such comparisons? What about the basic capability to live to a mature age, without succumbing to premature mortality?[283]

In fact, although it is not central to the thesis of his book, what Sen demonstrates with economic and sociological data is that comparatively, racialized poverty has a greater overall effect in North America than poverty in the Global South. It would seem, then, that the Occupy movement was onto something in their vocal criticism of the "one percent." The existence of vast riches, an outrageously high standard of living, and access to resources that thrive on the continued oppression of the unemployed and working poor results in much more catastrophic social consequences than economists originally understood.

Both the dominant and the marginalized in our society need to be liberated from systems of oppression. That requires interdependence. Interdependence involves recognizing the ways in which one person's affluence is built on another person's poverty. This is a risky thing to acknowledge. Becoming vulnerable and taking care of each other will mean that we could get hurt. We could get hurt when our communities fail to fulfill their intentions. We could get hurt when we expect to be treated the way we would treat another and that does not happen. But if we are to transform mission, we must learn interdependence.

Catherine Keller writes in *On the Mystery: Discerning Divinity in Process:* "Faith in these stories, in these relations of hearing, of risky self-disclosure, of facing fear, lets us step forward in mystery."[284] This is consistent with Cordova's writings on American Indian thoughts on "truth." Cordova argued that in many Indigenous societies there is an assumption that different cultures will have different experiences of truth, and that this is a natural phenomenon. The problem, as she saw it, is when "a culture has a sense only of *absolute* truth."[285] The possibility of relative truths, she wrote, is attacked by those who "are threatened by the idea that there might be different explanations for similar phenomena."[286] In my view, part of "facing fear" and "step[ping] forward into mystery," as Keller puts it, is to accept the seeming incommensurability of worldviews between Indigenous and dominant societies; indeed, I see the willingness to be vulnerable and to be transformed as moving towards Bosch's vision of what might be called an epistemology of participation.

One example of a church ministry that has made strides towards embodying solidarity and participation is Mennonite Church Canada's Indigenous ministries program. Steve Heinrichs, the former leader of this program, writes:

> For generations, Indigenous Peoples in Canada and the United States have been told by the government, church and businesses that there's an "Indian Problem," and that we Settlers can fix it through education, salvation, or economic development. But the disturbing truth is that the problems in Indian country have not been created by Indians. The problems, as Luther Standing Bear said, are "due to the white man's cast of mind." There's a "Settler problem," an ongoing colonialism that is ravaging Indigenous Peoples and the planet . . .
>
> This is not about demonizing white people, or inducing guilt; there are many morally outstanding white people (just as there were, no doubt, Ninevites). It's about confessing and resisting a system that perpetually privileges "white skin tones and European genetic lines"

> as it devours "whole people in its hungry economy and phobic gaze." It's about taking responsibility as "heirs of oppression."[287]

Here is a movement based in practice and experience. Mennonite Church Canada is helping facilitate the process of conscientization for Settler/Arrivant communities by encouraging their membership to take the risk of understanding their place in *Kanata's* racial and legal context. They are embodying a willingness to be transformed and led by Indigenous Peoples.

Cordova wrote, "A society that has power over another is not able to understand the matrix of the society over which it exercises power. The less powerful society's matrix, however, is constantly under attack. Through this attack both matrices are exposed."[288] This is why, at a time when the world is facing increased pressure through environmental degradation and an ever-increasing population, theology and, in particular, missiology, needs to open up to new worldviews and influences that will benefit the interdependence of all.

There is a colloquial maxim that defines insanity as doing the same thing over and over again, expecting different results. It is time for dominant societies to start listening to what Indigenous communities, who survived for tens of thousands of years prior to the conquest of the Americas, have to say about how the world can remain in balance.

In a recent article, Mark Laing asserts that Western worldviews still have enough influence over the global church to distract the churches at the margins from doing their own theological work. Echoing missiologist Richard Schenk, Laing states that this results in a theological agenda that requires intentional critical engagement and constructive theological effort to move in a direction that centres the marginalized.[289] This missional agenda is viewed as a possibility by Schenk, Bevans, Keller, and others. The relative invisibility of Indigenous concerns and voices in North American scholarship points to a different reality. As George Tinker notes, "It takes a great deal of intentional focus to break through the layers of colonial signification in order to begin to understand more accurately the contemporary situation for the aboriginal peoples of this continent."[290]

Theologian Joerg Rieger observes:

> The US is said to be more powerful now than Britain ever was. If mission and theology fail to develop an awareness of these developments and some insight into the close relation between authority and power, we will end up, once again, on the side of the powers that be, escaping the colonialist traps only to be caught in the neocolonialist ones. There is simply no "in-between" left in a globalizing world.[291]

This critique could well be applied to the continued colonization of North America, yet read in the context of this particular quote, it relates more overtly to the relationship between the United States and other nations. He did, however, address the colonization of North America in a later chapter "God and Power, Prophets and Native Lands" in *Theology that Matters*.[292] Rieger's commitment remains to building coalitions of solidarity across identity politics, and over time has taken decolonization seriously.

While critical theorists and African Studies scholars often draw attention to the racist fear that White blood would be contaminated or diluted through intermarriage, Tinker holds that the opposite is true when it comes to American Indians. He writes, "[the social policy strategy relating to intermarriage] was intended to include Indian peoples so that our lands and economic resources could be more easily taken away from us without the specter of guilt looming over the process."[293] One need only watch the 2023 film *Killers of the Flower Moon* to see how this played out in Osage country. This is precisely why Indigenous theology needs to remain political. Any transformation of Christian theology in general, and mission in particular, will have to first deal with the political ramifications of recognizing Indian claims to the land in North America as a precursor to initiating a non-colonial relationship between the dominant societies and the Indigenous Peoples of this land. Failure to do so would mean actively perpetuating systemic racial and economic injustice. As Vincent Donovan wrote, "The missionary should be an uncompromising adversary of injustice and oppression, an enemy of unjust structures and economic and social exploitation."[294] If we are to believe, as I do, that to be missional is to co-participate in *missio Dei*, then this work includes not only opposing unjust structures in the mission field (i.e. the Global South) but also in our own contexts here on this continent. Both the colonized and the colonizers must attempt to deconstruct the privileging of Whiteness and European descent that Heinrichs referred to earlier.

The Indigenous Peoples of North America hope to be received as valued contributors to theological discourse and to the church, not only because Indigenous people have been hurt (and continue to be hurt) by colonialism, but because *we all* have been hurt by colonialism. This is a truth Memmi, Freire, and others have identified; *all* people in society—both oppressors and oppressed—experience the consequences of oppression. The question that needs to be asked, then, is this: Is the church ready to receive us—Indigenous and marginalized, different as we may be—in order that *all* might be transformed? One would hope so.

I pray for the enactment of John Caputo's idea of "anarchic an-ethics."[295] An-ethics, according to Caputo, are based on biblical "strategic reversals" where the kingdom of God acts as a counterbalance to the kingdoms of the world. Where a traditional philosophical view of ethics sees the self as the agent, "the kingdom is organized around what the philosophers call 'heteronomy,' where responsibility means responding to the other," Caputo writes. He envisions a world in which "[o]ne takes oneself to be always already on the receiving end of the call of the other, always already solicited by the one who comes to me from on high just because he or she is laid low, like the man lying in the road whom the Samaritan encounters."[296] In other words, we come from a tradition of saying, "Here I am, God, send me."

This description of an anarchic an-ethics is congruent with Indigenous epistemologies in the sense that multiple truths are possible, and relationships and politics are of primary concern. More specifically, Caputo writes, "In the kingdom, responsibility implies heteronomy not autonomy, anarchy not autarchy, being held captive by the needs of the other, not the freedom to fill oneself up and satisfy one's needs."[297] If we focus on the heteronomy of communities (both Indigenous and Settler communities being subject to interaction with the other) rather than their autonomy, the relationship becomes interactive. Then Indigenous Peoples and Settlers are not seen as having competing truths and interests, but interactive truths and interests. There is a necessary symbiosis in our continued co-existence.

What could this look like? I heard a sermon once in an American church that left an impression. The pastor reflected on Amos 5 and Mark 10 in the context of the epidemic of mass-shootings in America schools. Towards the end of her sermon, she appealed to the congregation's patriotism by reminding us that the United States had been founded on justice and liberty "for all." As an Indigenous woman sitting in the congregation with my mother who is also Indigenous, I experienced an immediate visceral reaction to this repetition of a hegemonic cultural history founded on the Doctrine of Discovery.[298] Are the US and Canada founded on principles of truth, justice, and liberty for all? Not if you are Indigenous or someone whose ancestors were enslaved. Not if you are an undocumented worker paying taxes without representation or the possibility of legal residency or citizenship. How could this pastor have preached the same message in a way that showed solidarity with these communities? She could have acknowledged that while we haven't always lived up to the ideal of justice and liberty for all, it is still a founding principle to which we must hold ourselves accountable. This is what solidarity looks like.

This brings me to another argument that Caputo makes for heteronomy:

> Autonomy and freedom belong to the most classical assumptions of Greco-philosophical ethics, of onto-theo-logical ethical theory. In an anarchic an-ethics of alterity, *I worry that my freedom and autonomy pose a danger to the other, to those who are defenseless; for it is my freedom that keeps them out, that keeps them down, that threatens to kill them*" [emphasis mine].[299]

If Settler communities took this anarchic an-ethical approach, they would embody solidarity with Indigenous communities.

Mission as Quest for Justice

Thomas King's *The Inconvenient Indian: A Curious Account of Native People in North America* is lauded as witty, humourous, perceptive, and wise. King uses Indigenous epistemologies as a form of storytelling to reframe colonial history in North America. In the introduction he writes, "History may well be a series of stories we tell about the past, but the stories are not just any stories. They're not chosen by chance."[300] He goes on to say:

> When we imagine history, we imagine a grand structure, a national chronicle, a closely organized and guarded record of agreed-upon events and interpretations, a bundle of "authenticities" and "truths" welded into a flexible yet conservative narrative that explains how we got from there to here. It is a relationship we have with ourselves, a love affair we celebrate with flags and anthems, festivals and guns.
>
> Well, the "guns" remark was probably uncalled for and might suggest an animus toward history. But that's not true. I simply have difficulty with how we choose which stories become the pulse of history, and which do not.[301]

After a compelling, entertaining, infuriating, and discipline-crossing exploration of the history of colonization, King begins the second-to-last chapter with a question: "What do Indians want?"[302] He writes:

> But I'd just as soon forget the question entirely. There's a better question to ask. One that will help us to understand the nature of contemporary North American Indian history. A question we can ask of both the past and the present.
>
> What do Whites want?
>
> No, it's not a trick question. And I'm not being sarcastic. Native history in North America as writ has never really been about Native people. It's been about Whites and their needs and desires. What Native peoples wanted has never been a vital concern, has never been a political or social priority.[303]

His point is important for two reasons. It is bolstered by the arguments made by sociologist and professor of Black Studies George Lipsitz, mentioned previously, that dominant groups in society have a possessive investment in Whiteness.[304] It also frames the question about what constitutes justice in Indigenous-Settler relationships, especially if approached from Caputo's anarchic an-ethical approach to solidarity. But whether from an anarchic an-ethical approach or a classical Western approach, mission as quest for justice is a question worth exploring both politically and theologically.

I appreciate the definition of justice put forth by Paul Tillich in *Love, Power and Justice*. He writes that "justice was defined as the form in which power of being actualizes itself in the encounter of power with power."[305] The ontological nature of power—the inherent power of existence—is defined as justice or injustice by an analysis of the interaction of power with power. Cautioning us to avoid the compulsion to destroy (resulting in injustice), Tillich explains that to avoid injustice, "The answer must be: it is not compulsion which is unjust, but a compulsion which destroys the object of compulsion instead of working towards its fulfillment. It is not compulsion which violates justice, but a compulsion which disregards the intrinsic claim of a being to be acknowledged as what it is within the context of all beings."[306]

While this expression of interdependence and justice expressed by Tillich is congruent with the intercultural approach I propose, an expressly Indigenous perspective is presented by Taiaiake Alfred. In his Indigenous manifesto, *Peace, Power and Righteousness*, Alfred charges that dominant Western conceptions of justice are individualistic and materialistic.[307] He notes:

> By contrast, Indigenous notions of justice arose within the context of belief in a universal relationship among all the elements that make up our universe . . . Justice is seen as a perpetual process of maintaining that crucial balance and demonstrating true respect for the power and dignity of each part of the circle of interdependency.[308]

If justice is defined as a balance of inherent power and dignity of being with other beings, injustice is a type of dysfunction, according to Alfred.[309] Furthermore, the dysfunction or imbalance is not a simple contextual matter of occurrence, it's the context of imbalance and restoration that matters. Unlike Western legal conceptions of justice as right or wrong based on civil or common law, each imbalance of dysfunction must be examined contextually for resolution, not just imbalance:

> In the Indigenous view, determination of right and wrong cannot be abstracted from the particular context of the action or person in question,

> because re-establishing harmony requires not only consideration of all the elements concerned but their active participation in resolving the issue. That resolution involves dialogue, explanation, and repair of the fabric of the particular relationship—that is, healing. Justice is the process of healing relationships so that each element in creation can live its natural power and fulfil its responsibility.[310]

This relational, anarchic an-ethical Indigenous approach is supported by feminist theologies as well. The Greek concept *eros* refers to intimate love, but also life energy, the inherent power to *be*, as articulated by Alfred and Tillich. Rita Nakashima Brock writes that traditional patriarchal theologies examine power as unilateral, or power over the *other*. She argues for

> a christology not centered in Jesus, but in relationship and community as the whole-making, healing centre of Christianity . . . The reality of erotic power within connectedness means it cannot be located in a single individual. Hence what is truly christological, that is, truly revealing of divine incarnation and salvific power in human life, must reside in connectedness . . .[311]

Nakashima Brock is highlighting here the difference between a Jesus-centred Christology and a Christology that finds a Christic event in community. That communal sense of connection and eros becomes the path from justice-seeking to liberation. Nakashima Brock adds that "Heart—the self in original grace—is our guide into the territories of erotic power. Through that power we come to touch and be touched by, to transform and be transformed by all that is 'the whole and compassionate being.'"

Mission as Liberation

Given the church's roles in the oppression of Indigenous lives, one might ask: Why choose missiology at all? Why not walk away from the history and faith story of the church, of Christian faith? My answer is that I believe that mission can be a force for liberation. As imperfectly as it has been embodied by practitioners across all walks of life and strands of history, the salvific potential of Trinitarian faith is grounded in the hope that all can be transformed, that all can thrive and live in abundance. Mission includes our theologies (which I will come to in the next section), but also the actions we take in the world, actions inspired by and in the name of God and what we believe to be God's mission. Cultural theorist Chela Sandoval writes:

> The 1970s-80s social movement called US third world feminism functioned as a central locus of possibility, an insurgent social movement that shattered the construction of any one ideology as the single most correct site where truth can be represented . . . What US third world feminism thus demanded was a new subjectivity, a political revision that denied any one ideology as the final answer, while instead positing a tactical subjectivity with the capacity to de- and re-center, given the forms of power to be moved.[312]

This is related to the strategic essentialism identified by Gayatri Spivak,[313] although Spivak has faced criticism for the ways in which strategic essentialism can be used to grant permission for full-on essentialism. The tactical and strategic nature of Sandoval's theory is more defensible. She argues that women of colour do not have the luxury of acting on principle. She explains by quoting Cherríe Moraga: "Our strategy is how we cope . . . how we measure and weigh what is to be said and when, what is to be done and how, and to whom . . . daily deciding/risking who it is we can call an ally, call a friend (whatever that person's skin, sex or sexuality)."[314] In many ways, this book is a form of tactical subjectivity—every page is a choice to find opposition or alliance in the chorus of voices, both Indigenous and Settler, that precede my own.

The aim of these tactics, always, is liberation. Argentinian philosopher Enrique Dussel, informed by Indigenous worldviews and a life lived in conflict zones along class lines, picks up the themes of ethics and politics in his liberationist writings. In *Ethics of Liberation* he analyses the work of Nobel Peace Prize laureate Rigoberta Menchú[315] and the pedagogical models of Paulo Freire, before turning to what he calls the "emergence of new sociohistorical actors."[316] He writes: "Each ethical subject in everyday life, each concrete individual in all his or her acts, is already a possible subject of liberation praxis, insofar as he or she is a victim or solidary with the victim, and as such founds of norms, performs actions, organizes institutions or transforms ethnicity systems. The ethics of liberation is a possible ethics regarding any action of everyday life."[317] This includes considering the subject in the totality of their being—all the strategic tactics and essentialisms as represented by the whole *living* or *denied* subject.[318]

He explains that if one becomes acquainted with the "subject" of human life at the very deepest levels—

> [t]hus, Rigoberta Menchú's *feminine* "subject" (different by gender) is also the *Indian* subject (ethnicity), of *dark colour* (race), in devastated *lands* (ecological problems), *with no rights* (juridical exclusion), *no participation* in the dominated civil society (political), *poor* (economical), *peasant* (class), *illiterate* (formal culture), *Guatemalan* (a peripheral country), and so on. In each case, the "subjectivity" of the living *subject* has been "reduced" by a specific formality or refers to a performative systemic horizon, which can be seen abstractly (within formal "systems" as in Luhmann) and which are fetishized if one *judges* from them, as in the last instance, the *concrete living* subject, as only a "function" of the system. On the contrary, we must pass "transversally" from "the" concrete living subject (ultimate reference) to "all" possible functional subjectivities, as many levels of various systems of the subject that can intervene, *without the subject's being consumed by any of them* and *transcending* them always with a human living-ethical subject: as *the Other than any possible system*—"alterity" of all "totality," to express it in Levinas's critical metalanguage.[319]

For Dussel, the purpose of deep critical analysis of the intra-subjectivities of concrete living subjects is to highlight the possibility of transformation into liberation from those sociohistorical struggles. He highlights the famous statement of Marx from his *Theses on Feuerbach*: "Philosophers have only *interpreted* the world in differing ways; but the point is to *transform it*."[320] If we are to be transformed, theological enquiry and reflection must be an important part of the liberative process.

Conclusion

A word on postmodernism

IT COULD BE argued, based on some of the epistemological premises presented earlier in this book, that because Indigenous epistemology is primarily nondiscrete and nonbinary in nature, it is like the oft-critiqued positions of postmodernism that fail to reject universalism. In other words, Indigenous epistemologies lead to an unhelpful relativism. If this sounds dystopian, that may be because often when the dominant perspective encounters a vision of the world that does not seem to make sense, it casts it as frightening or undesirable. I believe that the backlash to postmodernity comes primarily from a fear grounded in White male privilege. White male privilege established the Western epistemological traditions and is invested in upholding them. I see this fear among the largely White middle class men who hold positions of authority within Western academic institutions, as well as among the mostly White women who have risen to positions of power within these institutions and who uphold the status quo. This is not to say that postmodernism should not be critiqued. But we could ask if there is not perhaps a more valuable critique of postmodernism than an accusation of relativism. For instance: In what ways does postmodernism lead to *re*-colonization?[321]

From an Indigenous and non-binary understanding of the world, there needs to be an appreciation of both the particular and the universal moral universe. This recognition leads us to the Indigenous question: What is the right path to walk? Postmodernism will only serve the healing of Indigenous and Settler communities (who benefit from our continued colonization) if we learn to benefit from the local experiences that are uplifted as a strength of postmodernism.

So far, that has not been the case. Sociologist Zygmunt Bauman writes: "What is wrong with the society we live in . . . is that it stopped questioning itself. This is a kind of society which no longer recognizes any alternative to itself and thereby feels absolved from the duty to examine, demonstrate, justify (let alone prove) the validity of its outspoken and tacit assumptions."[322] While the turn to the local or, even more, to the individual has resulted in much more outspoken critique than in the past, Bauman makes the point that "contemporary society has given 'hospitality to critique' an entirely new sense and has invented a way to accommodate critical thought and action while remaining immune to the consequences of that accommodation, and so emerging unaffected and unscathed—reinforced rather than weakened—from the tests and trials of the open-house policy."[323] This is, perhaps, what Sámi scholar Rauna Kuokkanen experienced at the Vancouver talk I wrote about in chapter two. While the gathering of educators purportedly intended to make space for Indigenous voices in education, it did not take long for the dominant perspective to reassert control. Worse still (and this dynamic is also identified by Bauman), despite their engaging presentations, the Indigenous plenary speakers were impotent in the face of rising hegemonic reactions from the audience to the possibilities for liberation that their presentations had opened.

Chela Sandoval argues for a "differential mode of social movement" in the face of a postmodern world. Building on Donna Haraway's "Manifesto for Cyborgs," Sandoval argues for the development of a "semiotic-material technology" (the linking of meanings and bodies) in order to develop a dissident form of globalization that is supported by technologies that "see from below" or from the perspective of the subjugated.[324] When one considers Raymond Willams's concept of "militant particularisms" as a critique of the ways in which place-based militant politics evolved in class struggles, I think it cannot apply here because most subjugated voices are less systematic. As Sandoval writes, "It has been assumed that the oppressed will behave without recourse to any *particular* method, or rather, that their behaviour consists of whatever acts one must commit in order to survive, whether physically or psychically."[325]

There are other supporters of epistemic pluralisms as they surface in postmodernism. In my own research, these supporters have appeared most prominently in theology, specifically in John Caputo's *What Would Jesus Deconstruct? The Good News of Postmodernism for the Church*[326] and in John R. Franke's *Manifold Witness: The Plurality of Truth*.[327] In particular, Franke is helpful in articulating why pluralist truth claims are not a challenge to overcome, but something to be celebrated. Although expressed in explicitly Christian language, I believe his position is commensurate with a nondiscrete, nonbinary Indigenous epistemology. He concludes his book *Manifold Witness* with these words:

> Plurality in the Christian community is not a problem to be overcome but is instead the very intention and blessing of God who invites all people to participate in the liberating and reconciling ministry of the gospel of Jesus Christ . . . We cannot bear this witness alone. We were never intended to do so. We need each other. It cannot be otherwise.[328]

Franke embraces the local particularisms as overlapping with the universal human experience of the divine through the Christian tradition. This aligns with an Indigenous epistemological perspective. Indigenous particularisms in epistemology do not seek to completely discount universalisms, but rather allow for the co-existence of the local with the universal.

The remaining question relates to the origins of Indigenous epistemologies. Are they about actually *existing* modes of thought among Indigenous Peoples, *historic* forms of thought that can be productively recovered, or *emerging* modes of thought in the process of dialogic and syncretic formation that are both unprecedented and built upon what some Medicine Wheel teachings call "original instructions"—the instructions passed on from Creator to people? I say yes to all three. I believe that Indigenous epistemologies are strategically employed as the embodiment of actually existing and unprecedented forms of thought also built upon original instructions.

It is easy to see where the history of colonization has created the "gaps" in knowledge identified by Anne Waters and other Indigenous philosophers I have mentioned. Vine Deloria Jr. states:

> For American Indians the period of opportunity [to discuss historical / traditional / uncontaminated Indigenous philosophy] probably ended for most tribes around 1900, when the last generation of people born free were in an elderly meditative stage of their lives.[329]

This would seem to suggest that it is not possible for discrete Indigenous perspectives to exist outside historical interaction with and influence by Western modes of thought. But in my view that is not problematic since Indigenous epistemologies are nondiscrete in the first place. What *actually exists* then is a survivor spirit that persists in the face of genocide and continued colonialism. This is not to be discounted.

I'm not convinced that Indigenous epistemologies represent a radical philosophical move, nor am I certain that what some might perceive to be the relativization of epistemology—if, in fact, this is what happens in comparing epistemic foundations—is a bad thing. Since there isn't a discipline of "Indigenous epistemologies," I have found that in attempting to define some epistemological variance from the heterodox Western epistemologies it has been helpful to look at the two general categories in relation to each other. Indigenous epistemologies are built on original instructions in the sense that contemporary Indigenous thought builds on what remains from Indigenous traditions and philosophies, despite intense efforts to assimilate and dispossess Indigenous people. While it would not be possible—based on Indigenous circular conceptions of history, tradition, community and grounded-ness in a particular place—to say that Indigenous epistemologies are "unprecedented," the *means* by which these epistemologies are being articulated, especially in twenty-first century scholarship, is certainly unprecedented.

Mission as "theology matters"

So often Settler society attempts—too quickly—to study, dissect, pathologize, solve, heal, and ultimately cleanse itself of what has been termed the "Indian Problem." At the same time, the question of land dispossession is either ignored or dismissed. Talking about land makes Settlers and Arrivants feel uncomfortable for many reasons. This dissonance is evidence of the epistemological hegemony Settler societies exert in their attempt to silence Indigenous voices because those voices necessarily challenge the political history of *Kanata* and the United States. Any discussion of land is quickly subsumed in an effort to eradicate difference. Left unchecked, this hegemonic drive will continue to ensure that Indigenous epistemologies remain disproven, discounted, fictional, anecdotal, and "inappropriately subjective" in an academy that is largely dominated by an epistemology grounded in Cartesian thought. I intended this work to be audacious in its politics. I claim most forthrightly and unabashedly that the politics of Indigenous theology matter. What we think about God and God's mission in the world matters, and it profoundly affects what we do or don't do.

Thia Cooper, translator of Enrique Dussel's *Politics of Liberation: A Critical World History*, identifies Dussel's work as "among the most important for constructing frameworks from which to reflect on liberative action . . . His work frames a structure that is critical to our understanding of the world and the possibilities for change."[330] Theologian Ivan Petrella writes in the preface to *Politics of Liberation* that "Liberation theologies were born with the promise of being theologies that would not rest with talking about liberation and instead would actually further liberation."[331] This is because:

> Liberation theologies are born from . . . struggles that were translated into an epistemological break with the whole of the Western theological tradition; that is, they are not one theological school among others in the canon. Instead they sought and seek a new understanding of theology itself.[332]

This brings us to the final theme in my quest for an Indigenous approach to missiology: mission as theology.

Scholars in the field hold diverse positions on the definition and praxis of *missio Dei.* While constructive and systematic theologies are starting to engage the concerns raised by anti-colonial and postcolonial theories and methodologies, comparatively little of this type of scholarship can be found in the field of missiology. As missiologists struggle with how to reconcile the Great Commission in Matthew 28 ("Go therefore and make disciples of all nations") with other calls to be a co-missioned people in the world (called by God to carry out God's mission), mainline Protestants until recently appeared to have lost some of their enthusiasm for mission and evangelism. The problem, in my view, is twofold.

First, "evangelical" can be a pejorative term in contemporary mainline churches. Evangelism and mission have always been closely linked. As mainline churches become more sensitive to postcolonial concerns, they are reluctant to speak of evangelism lest cultural imperialism influence how they share the gospel. The rapid growth of Evangelical churches in the world, especially churches whose theology is exclusivist, both challenges and vexes the mainline Protestant churches who find themselves in situations of decline. We envy their numbers and resources yet disdain what they teach about the Gospel. This is especially interesting to me given the wave of revivalism that swept North American Protestantism in the mid-to-late nineteenth century and preceded today's more charismatic contemporary evangelical traditions.

I am drawn to anti-colonialism and postcolonialism because they present liberatory possibilities for Indigenous Peoples in ways that have not been explicitly explored in the field of missiology to date. More broadly, anti-colonialism and postcolonial theory when applied to mission have the potential to be liberating for all people on the margins, not only in critiquing the "help" given through churches and their members, but in terms of recognizing the inherent power and worth of all beings in relation to each other.

I want to remind my readers here that although postcolonialism and other theologies from the margins present strong critiques of unjust *systems,* as a Christian I am always undertaking my critique with humility and as a revolutionary act of love towards my fellows. Paulo Freire argued in *Pedagogy of the Oppressed* that to work for liberation not only recognizes the humanity in the oppressed, but also uncovers the humanity of the oppressor. But that love needs to extend to "the least of these." Unless the marginalized are loved and loving, there can be no hope for humanity's liberation. I undertake this work with a profound sense of hope that although Christian faith has been harnessed to perpetuate both silent and explicit oppressions in the name of God, the truth-telling of postcolonial and anti-colonialism approaches will liberate us all.

Reclaiming missio Dei

This book has been an attempt to address three particularly tenacious dynamics in Indigenous and Settler/Arrivant relationships in contemporary North America. First, in the church and in society more broadly, what the dominant society has "given" to oppressed communities has always been conditional; aid has always come with strings attached, such as expectations of conformity or assimilation. Second, dialogue between dominant and marginalized communities, under traditional Western epistemological influence, has always been about solving problems rather than building relationships, and then only on terms that serve the interests of Settler/Arrivant communities. Lastly, the dominant economic order assumes that there is competition for scarce resources, while Indigenous epistemologies in general see the world and its economies as sources of abundance from which one only takes what one needs because there will always be more. This view plays out in a radical inclusivity that accepts those who are *other*, or beyond one's community.

The intercultural theology I have proposed challenges those three premises in the following ways: First, societies made up of Indigenous Peoples and Settlers (or any societies of dominant and oppressed) cannot continue to operate on dependency models whereby the oppressed have only the freedoms they are granted by the oppressor. Second, oppressors and oppressed must have equitable[333] access to resources and the terms of engagement must be reimagined as if there are enough resources and enough truths for all. Lastly, intercultural theology proposes that dialogue is an end itself, not a means to an end. In this way, the work of examining the power dynamics in Indigenous–Settler or oppressed–oppressor relationships becomes a process of conscientization. The oppressed become aware of the structures that force their oppression and convert from being sinned-against, and the oppressors become aware of their complicity in those oppressing structures and convert from sinning. Both groups must be liberated, and both must be converted. And so, we understand that *metanoia* and *koinonia* belong together.

The concept of *missio Dei* was originally intended to liberate the theology of mission from its tendency to reinforce the systems and structures of colonialist oppressors. But during the second half of the twentieth century *missio Dei* only incorporated the worldviews and the theological perspectives of American and European theologians whose efforts to address inequity stopped at multiculturalism and tolerance. But rather than giving up on the concept, as Philip Wickeri and others recommend, I believe that we are now closer than ever to being able to articulate some of the divine mystery which we can contemplate through *missio Dei* as a theological construct. From an Indigenous perspective, *missio Dei* must incorporate nonbinary and nondualist approaches to our theologizing; there is not just one right way to define God's mission. The mission of God must also be grounded in right action—towards the earth and towards each other—with our histories, stories, cultures, and values. If *missio Dei* is understood, not as a systematic concept but as a constructive call to right action, and is expressed in all the wondrous diversity of the world—stories, songs, art, the natural world, theology, liturgy, preaching, and prayer—our relationships will benefit and we may, with God's grace, be transformed towards liberation and justice.

For Further Reading

GIVEN THAT INDIGENOUS epistemology is not a discipline in itself, and that I am drawing from a number of transdisciplinary sources, I include here a summary of some of the more important works I use throughout the book. I have grouped the works surveyed into disciplinary approaches presented by Indigenous (and other) scholars and I explain why and how each group contributes to the project of healing the harms of colonialism and racism.

Benevolent predecessors

This body of work represents forerunners to contemporary Indigenous thought. These scholars are the critical theorists, postcolonial scholars, educators, and philosophers. Indigenous scholars have drawn upon their radical research for strength and precedent. The works in this group have been most formative in my recent research and writing. *Pedagogy of the Oppressed* by Paulo Freire (1968; translated by Myra Bergman Ramos, 1970; 30th anniversary edition, Continuum, 2003) continues to be for me, as for many others, a canonical work to which I turn repeatedly for guidance. This is the work that has most profoundly influenced the continual discovery of my own voice and experience. Freire writes:

> The radical, committed to human liberation, does not become the prisoner of a "circle of certainty" within which reality is also imprisoned. On the contrary, the more radical the person is, the more fully he or she enters into reality so that, knowing it better, he or she can better transform it. This individual is not afraid to confront, to listen to the

> world unveiled. This person is not afraid to meet people or to enter into dialogue with them. This person does not consider himself or herself the proprietor of history or of all people, or the liberator of the oppressed; but he or she does commit himself or herself, within history, to fight at their side. (39)

The basic premise of *Pedagogy of the Oppressed* is that popular education which links the lived experience of oppressed people to their awakening consciousness (a process Freire calls "conscientization") of systemic racism, economic exploitation, and sexism is necessary for the liberation of both the oppressed and the oppressor. He argues that neither oppressed nor oppressors are liberated unless *both* oppressed and oppressors are liberated. For this reason I believe my work is very much Freirian: dedicated to the consciousness-raising of both Indigenous and dominant communities, as well as to dialogue, interculturalism, and transformation in service of true liberation.

The Colonizer and the Colonized by Albert Memmi (1957; translated by Howard Greenfeld, 1965; expanded edition, Beacon Press, 1991) also remains a classic text that is appropriate in the context of this work. Memmi, a Jewish-Tunisian psychologist, wrote his controversial examination of the psychological dynamics of the colonizer and the colonized in the context of northern Africa, then under the colonial control of France and Belgium. Later in his career he wrote *Decolonization and the Decolonized* (2004; translated by Robert Bononno, University of Minnesota Press, 2006). In his 2006 update of this book, he offers a critique of the ways decolonization has failed in post-colonial contexts, partly because of colonizer resistance but also because of the failures of the colonized to claim integrity in their liberation. *The Colonizer and the Colonized*, however, has remained controversial because of its influence on some of the most militaristic liberation movements in colonized contexts, especially on the African continent. He writes, "I was told that in many parts of the world the colonial police confiscated the book in the cells of militant nationalists. I am convinced that I gave them nothing they did not already know, had not already experienced" (ix). I include his work in this canon of benevolent predecessors because everything in Memmi's articulation of the colonized experience in northern Africa can be recognized in other colonized Indigenous contexts that persist today.

Frantz Fanon's *Black Skin, White Masks* (1952; translated by Richard Philcox, Grove Press, 2008) and *The Wretched of the Earth* (1961; translated by Constance Farrington, Grove Press, 1965; and by Richard Philcox, Grove Press, 2004) are equally important in the history of colonization from the perspective of the marginalized and colonized. Like Memmi, Fanon wrote from the context of North Africa under French colonial rule. Fanon writes, "Our sole concern was to put to an end a vicious cycle. Fact: some Whites consider themselves superior to Blacks. Another fact: some Blacks want to prove at all costs to the Whites the wealth of the black man's intellect and equal intelligence. How can we break the cycle?" (xiv).

Fanon wrote about race, land, and economics in the context of colonization. Both of these books offer a radical revisionist agenda. Like Memmi's work, Fanon's writings attracted the attention of colonial authorities because of their potential to incite violence. In *Peace, Power and Righteousness: An Indigenous Manifesto* (Oxford University Press, 1999), Kahnawà:ke (Mohawk) writer Taiaiake Alfred also examines the colonial experience in ways that allow for violent upheaval, while suggesting that there are cultural approaches for both the colonizer and the colonized that can avoid violence. Reading Memmi and Fanon in parallel with Alfred shows how little societies have changed over the course of three quarters of a century of struggle against colonization.

The Idea of Latin America by Walter Mignolo (Blackwell, 2005) is an important resource for Indigenous researchers and writers. Mignolo shows how American and European discourse that uses the homogenous term "Latin America" erases both the Indigenous people of African descent living in the Americas as well as the forty million Latinx peoples in the US (something I'm guilty of). Mignolo writes within the framework of what Arturo Escobar called the modernity/coloniality research project, centering around the following six premises:

> 1. There is no modernity without coloniality, because coloniality is constitutive of modernity.
> 2. The modern/colonial world (and the colonial matrix of power) originates in the sixteenth century, and the discovery/invention of America is the colonial component of modernity whose visible face is the European Renaissance.
> 3. The Enlightenment and the Industrial Revolution are derivative historical moments consisting in the transformation of the colonial matrix of power.
> 4. Modernity is the name for the historical process in which Europe began its progress toward world hegemony. It carries a darker side: coloniality.
> 5. Capitalism, as we know it today, is of the essence for both the conception of modernity and its darker side, coloniality.
> 6. Capitalism and modernity/coloniality had a second historical moment of transformation after World War II when the US took the imperial leadership previously enjoyed at different times by both Spain and England. (xiii)

Especially important in his analysis is the idea of *coloniality*. Like Anne Waters's use of *Indigenist* as a way of thinking that is defined by a particular perspective and not by Indigenous identity, Mignolo's *colonialist* thinking is defined by a way of thinking and not the actual or persistent presence of a colony:

> The "invention of America" thesis offers . . . a perspective from coloniality and, in consequence, reveals that the advances of modernity outside of Europe rely on a colonial matrix of power that includes the renaming of the lands appropriated and of the people inhabiting them . . . While "colonialism" refers to specific historical periods and places of imperial domination . . . "coloniality" refers to the logical structure of colonial domination underlying the Spanish, Dutch, British and US control of the Atlantic economy and politics, and from there the control and management of almost the entire planet. (6-7)

The idea of coloniality persists in modern-day Canada and the United States, where colonization is so complete that one cannot conceive of a post-colonial context, only a context in which post-coloniality has reshaped the discourse of history, politics, and the economy.

In *Methodology of the Oppressed* (University of Minnesota Press, 2000), Chela Sandoval places what she terms a "US Third World Feminism" at the center of her world to theorize social movements for justice seeking. She is best known for critiquing feminisms for the ways in which they fail to acknowledge how race, class, and sex inform ideas of gender. She writes, "*Methodology of the Oppressed* is not organized as a history that recounts stages text by text while demonstrating forms of exchange that occur within each era. Rather, it is concerned with a general economy of consciousness in its oppositional forms." By examining late-twentieth-century critical theory, Sandoval reads poststructuralists alongside popular social activism to "discover new ways of reading, thinking, behaving, hoping, imagining, from the simplest activity . . . to the most obtuse, understanding the differential form of oppositional consciousness and social movement as the methodology of the oppressed that can generate a hermeneutics of love in the postmodern world" (10-11). See also her essay "US Third World Feminism: The Theory and Method of Oppositional Consciousness in the Postmodern World," in *Genders* 10 (Spring 1991), 1-24.

Some other important sources for Indigenist researchers and writers are postcolonial theorists Homi Bhaba (*The Location of Culture,* Routledge, 2004; *Nation and Narration,* Routledge, 1990; and, with Robert J.C. Young, *White Mythologies,* Routledge, 2004); Gayatri Spivak (*A Critique of Postcolonial Reason: Toward a History of the Vanishing Present,* Harvard University Press, 1999; *In Other Worlds: Essays in Cultural* Politics, Routledge, 2006; and, with Sarah Harasym, *The Post-Colonial Critic: Interviews, Strategies, Dialogues,* Routledge, 1990); Edward Said (*Orientalism,* Vintage, 1979; and *Culture and Imperialism,* Vintage, 1994); Bill Ashcroft (*Post-Colonial Transformation,* Routledge, 2001); and *Post-Colonial Studies: The Key Concepts,* edited by Ashcroft, Gareth Griffiths, and Helen Tiffin, Routledge, 1998). The works of these postcolonial writers are useful to Indigenous scholars because they have laid the foundations for a platform from which the subaltern attempts to speak. (See Gayatri Spivak, "Can the Subaltern Speak?" in *Marxism and the Interpretation of Culture*, edited by Cary Nelson and Lawrence Grossberg, University of Illinois Press, 1988, 271-316.)

If Indigenous epistemologies are unbounded, nondiscrete, and nonbinary in nature and attempt to include a holistic perspective of human experience, then drawing on the work of other epistemologically marginalized works is not only allowable but also appreciated from an Indigenist point of view.

Old school "Native exclusivism"

By "old school Native exclusivism" I refer to the important yet overly-essentialist work of pioneers in the field of Native scholarship. This would include scholars like Vine Deloria Jr. (*Custer Died for Your Sins: An Indian Manifesto*, University of Oklahoma Press, 1969; and *God is Red: A Native View of Religion,* 30th anniversary edition, Fulcrum, 2003) and Donald Fixico (*The American Indian Mind in a Linear World: American Indian Studies and Traditional Knowledge*, Routledge, 2003). They, along with their brothers (for they were mostly men), were the first American Indian/First Nations scholars to attain academic notoriety for their controversial views. Their scholarship, inspired by the identity politics movements that developed in the wake of Native enfranchisement in north America, portrayed the militancy of the American Indian Movement and other political groups. In the tradition of Memmi and Fanon, Deloria Jr. and others wrote manifestos on the state of Native America in order to raise a call for "Indians" to liberate themselves from colonialism and to confront the mainstream denial of the history of colonization in North America. One problem with the writings of these men is that they, like many non-Native writers at a time, did not yet fully appreciate the influence of second wave feminism on the academy. They did not use gender-inclusive language in their scholarship, and they excluded anyone they deemed to be "inauthentic" Indians. Fixico endorsed a hierarchy of blood quantum, and Deloria Jr. judged "off-rez" Indians as being somehow "tainted" by White American systems of thought and therefore less "Native." This type of exclusivism is less evident—though not completely eradicated—in contemporary Native thought, as can be seen in the more recent work of Anne Waters (editor of *American Indian Thought: Philosophical Essays*, Blackwell, 2004), Brian Yazzie Burkhart (see "What Coyote and Thales Can Teach Us" in *American Indian Thought*), and others. While the writings of scholars like Deloria Jr. and Fixico contain certain hypocrisies, they should not be discounted; their methodologies and strategies of resistance paved the way for successive generations of Indigenous scholarship in North America, including my own. They opened the eyes of both Native and non-Native people to the fact that the status quo continues to be unacceptable and there is much left to heal in Indigenous/non-Indigenous relationships.

Manifestos

These are works by scholars who write from entirely Indigenous perspectives. I include among them political theorist Taiaiake Alfred's *Peace, Power and Righteousness: An Indigenous Manifesto* (Oxford University Press, 1999), and *Wasáse: Indigenous Pathways of Action and Freedom* (University of Toronto Press, 2005). Manifestos are political declarations of intention or calls to action. Calvin Helin's *Dances with Dependency* (Orca Spirit Publishing, 2006) is manifesto-like in its call to First Nations in Canada to confront their acceptance of the dependency model perpetuated by the state. Where I disagree with Helin is his unapologetic embrace of neo-liberal capitalism, especially as expressed in full support for Indigenous mining and oil and gas industries, which I view to be harmful to God's created order. I would also include *Indigenizing the Academy*, edited by Devon Mihesuah and Waziyatawin Angela Wilson (Bison Books, 2004), as well as *For Indigenous Eyes Only: A Decolonization Handbook*, edited by Waziyatawin Angela Wilson and Michael Yellow Bird (School of American Research Press, 2005). While I find the works in this genre to be provocative and probably too essentialist for my liking (I prefer the more nuanced work of the Native American philosophers), their radical political ideas attempt to counter Indigenous nihilism and inspire hope that another future is possible, even if that future looks radically different from a romanticized Indigenous past.

Historical revisions

In this category I include Indigenous and non-Indigenous allies who seek to retell history, however imperfectly, either from an Indigenous perspective or at least one inclusive of Indigenous realities. From Indigenous writers, this would include most notably Georges Sioui's *Huron Wendat: The Heritage of the Circle* (translated by Jane Brierley, UBC Press, 2005) and *For an Amerindian Autohistory: An Essay on the Foundations of a Social Ethic* (translated by Sheila Fischman, McGill-Queen's University Press, 1992). In both works, Sioui tells the histories of his people using multiple forms such as stories that connect the past, present, and future interwoven with moral teachings from his Huron cultural perspective.

Thomas King's *The Inconvenient Indian: A Curious Account of Native People in North America* (University of Minnesota Press, 2012) is another, and perhaps more accessible, retelling of the history of colonization and the colonialist present of Canada and the US. King is not a professor of history, but rather of literature, and this can be seen in his style:

> As a result, although *The Inconvenient Indian* is fraught with history, the underlying narrative is a series of conversations and arguments that I've been having with myself and others for most of my adult life, and if there is any methodology in my approach to the subject, it draws more on storytelling techniques than historiography. A good historian would have tried to keep biases under control. A good historian would have tried to keep personal anecdotes in check. A good historian would have provided footnotes.
>
> I have not.
>
> And, while I'm making excuses, I suppose I should also apologize if my views cause anyone undue stress. But I hope we can agree that any discussion of Indians in North America is likely to conjure up a

> certain amount of rage. And sorrow. Along with moments of irony and humor. (xii)

This work, probably more than any other on the subject, represents to me the embodiment of history from an Indigenous epistemological perspective. No longer confined by the boundaries of western historiography, King uses superb storytelling techniques for both pedagogical and ethical purposes. He conveys the Native experience in a way that causes Indigenous readers to see themselves in the text and non-Indigenous readers to care about Indigenous histories.

From non-Native allies in the field of history, I would include Geoffrey York's *The Dispossessed: Life and Death in Native Canada* (Vintage, 1990), Cole Harris's *Making Native Space: Colonialism, Resistance, and Reserves in British Columbia* (UBC Press, 2003), and Susan Neylan's *The Heavens Are Changing: Nineteenth-Century Protestant Mission and Tsimshian Christianity* (McGill-Queen's University Press, 2003). These more nuanced readings of history are important to the project of making history more representative of Indigenous experience. More importantly, they start to deconstruct the hegemonic assumptions upon which the narratives of the foundations of Canada and the United States were built.

Education and education reform

This body of work has two purposes. The first is to examine the epistemological underpinnings of Indigenous education. The second is to explore the delivery of adequate, culturally relevant education to Native students and the preservation and teaching of traditional forms of knowledge and language. Notable works in this genre (besides Fixico) are the aforementioned *Indigenizing the Academy*, edited by Mihesuah and Wilson, as well as *Reshaping the University: Responsibility, Indigenous Epistemes, and the Logic of the Gift* by Rauna Kuokkanen (UBC Press, 2007), *Red Pedagogy: Native American Social and Political Thought* by Sandy Grande (Rowman & Littlefield, 2004), *Protecting Indigenous Knowledge and Heritage*, edited by Marie Battiste and James Sa'Ke'j Youngblood Henderson (Purich Publishing, 2000), and

Making Space for Indigenous Feminisms, edited by Joyce Green (Zed Books, 2008). Some additional pedagogical approaches present historical revisions and curriculum designs based on Indigenous epistemologies: *Tsawalk: A Nuu-chah-nulth Worldview* by Richard Atleo (UBC Press, 2004), *Wasáse* by Taiaiake Alfred, and the works of Gregory Cajete, including *Look to the Mountain* (Kivaki Press, 1994) and *Igniting the Sparkle* (Kivaki Press, 2000). I would also include Linda Tuhiwai Smith's *Decolonizing Methodologies* (Zed Books, 1999). This is probably the field with the most extensive Indigenous bibliography.

In my view, education reform remains one of the most important vehicles for healing. My views on this were shaped by an experience I had in 2004 during a class trip to Guatemala. We visited the *Fundación Nueva Esperanza* (New Hope Foundation) school in Rabinal. There I witnessed the effects of epistemologically and culturally relevant curriculum and course design for Indigenous students. Under the leadership of Jesús Tecu, a Mayan Achi leader, the Foundation had established a new program based on Achi ethics and epistemologies. Although Rabinal was the site of some of the most horrific violence in the history of armed struggle in Guatemala, the children in this school were bright-eyed and full of life and hope. This provided a stark contrast to what I often observe among Indigenous children in Canada. If education reform for Indigenous (and non-Indigenous) children in Canada could follow a model similar to the one used in Rabinal, this would give me much hope for a future of healing between Indigenous and Settler/Arrivant communities in Canada.

Indigenous spiritualties and psychologies

Indigenous authors have written enough works about religious spiritualties and psychologies to fill many more essays. I find George "Tink" Tinker's writing to be the most helpful in reframing Christian theology from an Indigenous epistemological point of view, especially in his two later works, *Spirit and Resistance: Political Theology and American Indian Liberation* (Fortress Press, 2004) and *American Indian Liberation: A Theology of Sovereignty* (Orbis,

2008). Tinker's theological arguments hold great value, especially when augmented with Indigenist philosophical approaches. Another volume on this topic is *Religion and Healing in Native America: Pathways for Renewal*, edited by Suzanne J. Crawford O'Brien (Praeger Publishers, 2008). O'Brien presents the lived experience of Native communities using traditional (i.e. non-Christian) perspectives on healing and religion to re-orient themselves toward their communities and the surrounding environment. This work is particularly helpful for Indigenous readers or for people who work with Indigenous people in need of healing.

Two other books on the topic of healing are relevant here. *In the Realm of Hungry Ghosts: Close Encounters with Addiction* by Gabor Maté (North Atlantic Books, 2008) shows how addictions result from emotionally empty childhoods. Maté worked in Vancouver's Downtown Eastside, a neighbourhood with a high Indigenous population and many residents who experience homelessness, poverty, mental health issues, and addictions. His work addresses one of the most pressing areas in need of healing in Indigenous life: addictions. Healing is needed for individuals, families, and communities. Maté's work isn't specifically aimed at Indigenous people, which is appropriate because addiction is not a solely racialized problem; people of all races, backgrounds, and socio-economic status experience this struggle. Finding healing in this realm could create a point of connection between Indigenous and non-Indigenous communities.

Another important work in this field is Eduardo Duran's recent *Healing the Soul Wound: Counseling with American Indians and Other Native Peoples* (Teacher's College Press/Columbia University, 2006). Duran's case studies present healing strategies for Indigenous peoples, addressing substance abuse, intergenerational trauma, and internalized oppression.

These two important sources present approaches to healing what Duran describes as the "soul wound" many Indigenous people suffer from. Native communities have statistically higher levels of addictions and mental illnesses associated with long-time substance use and Fetal Alcohol Spectrum Disorders. No matter how much Indigenous critical theory or epistemological philosophy is developed by Indigenous scholars, we must deal with the very real and pressing concerns of those who are suffering from the continued trauma of displacement, racism, poverty, and abuse that is so pervasive in Indigenous communities, both urban and rural, on- and off-reserve. To illustrate the effects of the "soul wound" and why it is important in Native scholarship, I end this section with a sad but favourite quote by novelist Lee Maracle, from *Daughters Are Forever* (Raincoast Books, 2002).

> Grace has left their bodies. They are rendered stiff and tense by the knot of shame that sits stuck in their throats. It needs to be expressed, pushed up and out so they may sing again, but five centuries of "Hush, don't cry" holds the expression of their shame still. Under it lies a dangerous grief. They now tread heavily upon the back of their mother. Lunging from place to place, they plant seeds but don't bother to watch them grow. They water nothingness as though this water will somehow recreate life without their participation. Many have acquired the jerky movements, the bad skin, and the hard, strident song-less voices of the newcomers. Their world has lost its future. Cut off from considering their past, they list in the momentary context of the present. Consideration requires a spiritual sensibility, one that sees life from all its jewel-like angles. [They] don't see life; they barely feel their existence. They avert each other's gaze. The reflection of grief and shame in the eyes of others mirrored back at them is too terrifying to contemplate. They mark time. Time is the enemy of the dispirited. [They] wander aimlessly, killing time in small pieces. (25)

Notes

1 Kinnie Starr, Rifles," *How I Learned to Run: Poetry, Illustrations & Photographs* (House of Parlance Media, 2008), 46-47.

2 See Paulo Freire, *Pedagogy of the Oppressed,* 30th anniversary ed. (Bloomsbury Academic, 2000).

3 Enrique Dussel, *Politics of Liberation: A Critical World History,* Thia Cooper, translator (SCM Press, 2011), xiii.

4 I first became aware of this concept as introduced in Nelson Maldonado-Torres, *Against War: Views from the Underside of Modernity* (Duke University Press, 2008). Maldonado-Torres, influenced by Dussel among others, was my introduction to scholars who managed to allow contextual diversity in the global common experience of oppression in a very powerful and articulate way.

5 Dussel, *Politics of Liberation*, 2.

6 See the work of feminist theologians Rita Nakashima Brock and Rebecca Parker, as well as most Latina and Womanist theologians. Specifically see Rita Nakashima Brock and Rebecca Parker, *Of Proverbs and Ashes: Violence and Redemptive Suffering and the Search for What Saves Us* (Beacon Press, 2002).

7 See the section "A Note on Style" for a fuller explanation of my use of this term.

8 Carolyn Ellis, *The Ethnographic I: A Methodological Novel about Autoethnography* (Altamira Press, 2004), xix.

9 See Carolyn Ellis, *The Ethnographic I,* chapter 6.

10 Ruth Behar, *The Vulnerable Observer: Anthropology that Breaks Your Heart* (Beacon Press, 1996), 14.

11 See Andrea Smith, *Conquest: Sexual Violence and American Indian Genocide* (South End Press, 2005).

12 See Cornel West, *Race Matters,* 2nd ed. (Vintage, 2001).

13 See Jione Havea, "The Cons of Contextuality . . . Kontextuality," in *Contextual Theology for the Twenty-First Century*, ed. Stephen B. Bevans and Katalina Tahaafe-Williams (Pickwick Publications, 2011), 44. Jenny Te Paa asks a similar question in her chapter entitled "Contexts, Controversy, and Contradiction in Contemporary Theological

Education: Who Bene 'Fits' and Who Just Simply Doesn't Fit?" in the same volume, 69-86.

14 For more explanation of the term Indigenist, see *American Indian Thought: Philosophical Essays*, ed. Anne Waters (Blackwell, 2004).

15 "NIH Style Guide," National Institutes of Health, https://www.nih.gov/nih-style-guide/race-national-origin.

16 The name Canada (*Kanata*) came from the Huron-Iroquoian word *kanata*, meaning village or settlement.

17 For a full text of the United Church apology, see "The Apologies," https://united-church.ca/social-action/justice-initiatives/reconciliation-and-indigenous-justice/apologies.

18 I am a member of the *Haíɫzaqv* First Nation. Our legal governance structure under *The Indian Act* in *Kanata* refers to us as the Heiltsuk Tribal Council. Heiltsuk is an anglicization of *Haíɫzaqv*, and so in this book I use the term *Haíɫzaqv* Tribal Council.

19 See "Haíɫcístut: Our Path to True Reconciliation," https://heiltsuknation.ca/our-path-to-true-reconciliation/.

20 See "Historic Pain and the Political Present" in George Tinker, *American Indian Liberation: A Theology of Sovereignty* (Orbis Books, 2008), 1-16.

21 Tinker, *American Indian Liberation*, 2.

22 Gustavo Gutiérrez, *A Theology of Liberation: History, Politics and Salvation*, 15th anniversary ed. (Orbis Books 1988), 20.

23 Daniel Harnett, "Remembering the Poor: An Interview with Gustavo Gutierrez," *America: The National Catholic Review*, http://americamagazine.org/issue/420/article/remembering-poor-interview-gustavo-gutierrez.

24 Catherine Keller, *On the Mystery: Discerning Divinity in Process* (Fortress Press, 2008), 9.

25 Keller, *On the Mystery*, 12.

26 Keller, *On the Mystery*, 13.

27 Chris Budden, "The Necessity of a Second People's Theology in Australia," in *Contextual Theology for the Twenty-First Century*, eds. Stephen B. Bevans and Katalina Tahaafe-Williams (Pickwick Publications, 2011), 61.

28 Julie Thompson Klein, *Interdisciplinarity: History, Theory and Practice* (Wayne State University Press, 1990), 78.

29 Judith Berling, "Models of Interdisciplinarity" (handout in IDS 6000 seminar class at the Graduate Theological Union, Berkeley, Fall 2008), 3.

30 I understand systematic theology to be the study and practice of theology that attempts to "systematize" theological thought based on traditionally defined categories. For example: Definition of God, theological anthropology (what God intends for humans), Christology, pneumatology, soteriology, etc.. Constructive theology, as I understand it,

pushes against the centering of those traditional categories and approaches the discipline of theology as constructed understandings of the past, but also engages in continued and ongoing construction of our theological understanding. Constructive theology acknowledges implicitly or explicitly that the theological endeavour is a construct.

31 David J. Bosch, *Transforming Mission: Paradigm Shifts in Theology of Mission* (Orbis Books, 1991).

32 George Tinker, *Missionary Conquest: The Gospel and Native American Cultural Genocide* (Fortress Press, 1993).

33 Tinker, *Missionary Conquest*, 5.

34 My ThM thesis was an in-depth exploration of Bosch's missiology. See Carmen Rae Lansdowne, "Humble Boldness/Bold Humility: Creative Tension and Power Analysis in Postcolonial Directions for Missiology in the 21st Century" (Vancouver School of Theology, 2011).

35 See Dale B. Martin, *Sex and the Single Saviour: Gender and Sexuality in Biblical Interpretation* (Westminster John Knox Press, 2006.)

36 Bosch, *Transforming Mission*, 349-62.

37 Willem A. Saayman and J.N.J. Kritzinger, eds., *Mission in Bold Humility: David Bosch's Works Considered* (Orbis Books, 1996).

38 Willem A. Saayman and J.N.J. Kritzinger, eds., *Mission in Creative Tension: A Dialogue with David Bosch* (S.A. Missiological Society, 1990).

39 Constance F. Parvey, *The Community of Women and Men in the Church: A Report of the World Council of Churches' Conference, Sheffield, England, 1981* (Fortress Press, 1983).

40 Vatican Secretariat for Christian Unity and World Council of Churches Commission on World Mission and Evangelism Joint Working Group, "Christian Witness—Common Witness," *New Directions in Mission and Evangelization 1: Basic Statements 1974-1991*, eds. James A. Scherer and Stephen B. Bevans (Orbis Books, 1992), 18-26.

41 See Cheri DiNovo, *Que(e)rying Evangelism: Growing the Church from the Outside In* (Pilgrim Press, 2005).

42 J. Jayakiran Sebastian, "Interrogating *missio Dei*: From the Mission of God towards Appreciating our Mission to God in Indian Today," in *News of Boundless Riches: Interrogating, Comparing and Reconstructing Mission in a Global Era*, vol. 1, ed. Max L. Stackhouse and Lalsangkima Pachuau (Indian Society for Promoting Christian Knowledge, 2007), 26-44.

43 Russell Means, in Ward Churchill, *A Little Matter of Genocide: Holocaust and Denial in the Americas 1492 to the Present* (City Lights Books, 1997), epigraph.

44 Ward Churchill, "Introduction," *A Little Matter of Genocide: Holocaust at Denial in the Americas 1492 to the Present* (City Lights Books, 1997), 4.

45 Tinker, *Missionary Conquest*, 5.

46 Tinker, *Missionary Conquest*, 5.

47 Stephen Neill, *A History of Christian Missions* (Penguin, 1990), 414.

48 Neill, *A History of Christian Missions*, 462.

49 Tinker, *Missionary Conquest*, 16.

50 Michael Omi, in George Lipsitz, *The Possessive Investment in Whiteness: How White People Profit from Identity Politics* (Temple University Press, 2006), 46.

51 George Lipsitz, *The Possessive Investment in Whiteness: How White People Profit from Identity Politics* (Temple University Press, 2006), 46.

52 David J. Bosch, in Joerg Rieger, "Theology and Mission Between Neocolonialism and Postcolonialism," *Mission Studies: Journal for the International Association for Mission Studies* 21, no. 2 (2004): 201.

53 Rieger, "Theology and Mission Between Neocolonialism and Postcolonialism."

54 Rieger, "Theology and Mission Between Neocolonialism and Postcolonialism," 202.

55 A more nuanced understanding of the colonial drive is offered by scholars like Ramón Grosfoguel, Enrique Dussel and others, who argue that the advent of colonialism was the conquest of Al-Andalus and the Andalusian genocide of Muslims in Spain that also started in the late 1490s.

56 Bill Ashcroft, Gareth Griffiths, and Helen Tiffin, eds., *Post-Colonial Studies: The Key Concepts* (Routledge, 2000), 186.

57 See Albert Memmi, *Decolonization and the Decolonized* (University of Minnesota Press, 2006).

58 Catherine Keller, Michael Nausner, and Mayra Rivera, eds., *Postcolonial Theologies: Divinity and Empire* (Chalice Press, 2004), 6.

59 Keller, Nausner, and Rivera, *Postcolonial Theologies*, 11.

60 Waziyatawin Angela Wilson and Michael Yellow Bird, eds., *For Indigenous Eyes Only: A Decolonization Handbook* (School of American Research, 2005), 2.

61 Statistics Canada, "Primary health care access among First Nations people living off reserve, Métis and Inuit, 2017 to 2020," https://www150.statcan.gc.ca/n1/pub/41-20-0002/412000022023005-eng.htm.

62 Statistics Canada, "Primary health care access among First Nations people living off reserve, Métis and Inuit, 2017 to 2020."

63 Canada, Indigenous Services Canada, "Annual Report to Parliament 2020," https://www.sac-isc.gc.ca/eng/1602010609492/1602010631711.

64 Canada, Parliamentary Research Branch, "Some Major Findings of the Report [Royal Commission on Aboriginal Peoples]," www.publications.gc.ca/Pilot/LoPBdP/EB/prb9924-e.htm.

65 Canada, Royal Commission on Aboriginal Peoples, *Report of the Royal Commission on Aboriginal Peoples Volume 5, Renewal: A Twenty-Year Commitment* (Minister of Supply

and Services Canada, 1996), 241-255.

66 Insight Canada Research, quoted in Dan Beavon and Jerry White, "Introduction," in *Aboriginal Well-being: Canada's Continuing Challenge*, ed. Jerry White, Dan Beavon and Nicholas Spence (Thompson Educational, 2007), 10.

67 Beavon and White, "Introduction," *Aboriginal Well-being*, 9. As of 2024, no similar data has been published based on the 2016 or 2021 Census.

68 See Bridget Stringer-Holden, "First Nations Life Expectancy Plunges, CBC British Columbia, August 21, 2024, https://www.cbc.ca/news/canada/british-columbia/first-nations-life-expectancy-plunges-by-6-years-in-b-c-report-1.7301471.

69 See White, Bevon, and Spence, *Aboriginal Well-being.*

70 Canada, Royal Commission on Aboriginal Peoples, *Report of the Royal Commission on Aboriginal Peoples, Volume 1, Looking Forward, Looking Back*, chapter 1, "Getting Started," http://central.bac-lac.gc.ca/.redirect?app=rcap&id=400&lang=eng.

71 Tom Flanagan, *First Nations? Second Thoughts* (McGill-Queen's University Press, 2000), 3.

72 Flanagan, *First Nations? Second Thoughts*, 5.

73 Flanagan, *First Nations? Second Thoughts*, 5.

74 See especially *First Nations, First Thoughts: The Impact of Indigenous Thought in Canada*, ed. Annis May Timpson (UBC Press, 2009).

75 Flanagan, *First Nations? Second Thoughts*, 195.

76 Michelle Reid, "Top 10 list: How not to respond to Indigenous experiences of racism in Canada," Rabble.ca, Sept. 4, 2013, https://rabble.ca/anti-racism/top-10-list-how-not-to-respond-to-indigenous-experiences-racism-canada/.

77 Taiaiake Alfred, *Peace, Power and Righteousness: An Indigenous Manifesto* (Oxford University Press Canada, 1999), xi-xii.

78 Eduardo Duran and Bonnie Duran, *Native American Postcolonial Psychology* (State University of New York Press, 1995), 29.

79 Duran and Duran, *Native American Postcolonial Psychology*, 1.

80 Geoffrey York, *The Dispossessed: Life and Death in Native Canada* (Vintage, 1990), xiii.

81 Canada, Royal Commission on Aboriginal Peoples, *Report of the Royal Commission on Aboriginal Peoples, Volume 5, Renewal*, 4.

82 See Albert Memmi, *The Colonizer and the Colonized*, expanded ed. (Beacon Press, 1991), and *Decolonization and the Decolonized* (University of Minnesota Press, 2006).

83 See Walter Mignolo, *The Idea of Latin America* (Blackwell, 2005).

84 See Mignolo, *The Idea of Latin America*, 6-11.

85 See Memmi, *The Colonizer and the Colonized.*

86 Memmi, *The Colonizer and the Colonized*, 52.

87 See Cornel West, *Race Matters* (Vintage, 2001). Specifically, Chapter 1, entitled "Nihilism

in Black America" where he states: "The liberal/conservative discussion [on conditions of life in Black America] conceals the most basic issue now facing black America: *the nihilistic threat to its very existence.* This threat is not simply a matter of relative economic deprivation and political powerlessness—though economic well-being and political clout are requisites for meaningful black progress. It is primarily a question of speaking to the profound sense of psychological depression, personal worthlessness, and social despair so widespread in black America" (19-20).

88 Memmi, *The Colonizer and the Colonized*, 52.

89 Memmi, *The Colonizer and the Colonized*, 53.

90 Andrea Smith, "Indigeneity, Settler Colonialism, White Supremacy," *Global Dialogue* 12, no. 2 (2010), http://www.worlddialogue.org/content.php?id=488.

91 Memmi, *The Colonizer and the Colonized*, 76.

92 See especially *American Indian Thought: Philosophical Essays,* ed. Anne Waters (Wiley Blackwell, 2004), V.F. Cordova, *How it Is: The Native American Philosophy of V.F. Cordova*, ed. Kathleen Dean Moore et al. (University of Arizona Press, 2007), Dale Turner, *This is Not a Peace Pipe: Towards a Critical Indigenous Philosophy* (University of Toronto Press, 2006), and Richard Atleo, *Tsawalk: A Nuu-chah-nulth Worldview* (UBC Press, 2004). In addition, other marginalized communities are starting to raise epistemological questions, such as the Latino/Latina studies volume *Decolonizing Epistemologies: Latino/a Theology and Philosophy* edited by Ada María Isasi-Díaz and Eduardo Mendieta (Fordham University Press, 2012).

93 Walter Mignolo, "Decolonizing Western Epistemology/Building Decolonial Epistemologies" in *Decolonizing Epistemologies: Latino/a Theology and Philosophy,* ed. Ada María Isasi-Díaz and Eduardo Mendieta (Fordham University Press, 2012), 22.

94 Ada María Isasi-Díaz and Eduardo Mendieta, "Introduction: Freeing Subjugated Knowledge" in *Decolonizing Epistemologies: Latino/a Theology and Philosophy,* ed. Ada María Isasi-Díaz and Eduardo Mendieta (Fordham University Press, 2012), 2.

95 Isasi-Díaz and Mendieta, "Introduction," 3.

96 David J. Bosch, *Transforming Mission*, 489.

97 Cordova, *How It Is*, 37.

98 Cordova, *How It Is*, 37.

99 Vincent J. Donovan, *Christianity Rediscovered*, 25th anniversary ed. (Orbis Books, 2003), 146.

100 Sebastian, "*Interrogating* missio Dei," 27.

101 Jodi A. Byrd, *The Transit of Empire: Indigenous Critiques of Colonialism* (University of Minnesota Press), xiii.

102 Philosophers have developed a discourse outlining that belief *P* has the (propositional) *content P*. The idea of justified true belief arises from the need to characterize those

contents and determining the characteristics of those characterizations. In other words, one believes P because that belief is made up of certain "contents" that constitute knowledge. Determining if that content is true or not will justify (or not) that belief.

103 John Greco, "Introduction: What is Epistemology?" ed. John Greco and Ernest Sosa, *The Blackwell Guide to Epistemology* (Blackwell, 1999), 1.

104 Nicholas Wolterstorff, "Epistemology of Religion," in *The Blackwell Guide to Epistemology*, ed. John Greco and Ernest Sosa (Blackwell, 1999), 307.

105 Wolterstorff, 307.

106 René Descartes, *Meditations*, 1641, John Veitch, translator (Cosimo Books, 2001), 73.

107 See "Meditation II: Of the Nature of the Human Mind, and That It Is More Easily Known than the Body" in Descartes, *Meditations*, 78-85.

108 John Carriero, *Between Two Worlds: A Reading of Descartes' Meditations* (University Press, 2009), 350-351.

109 Descartes in Carriero, 351.

110 John Locke, *An Essay Concerning Human Understanding*, 1689, abridged and edited by Raymond Wilburn (Dent, 1947), 252.

111 Locke, *An Essay Concerning Human Understanding*, 326.

112 David Hume, *An Enquiry Concerning Human Understanding*, 1748, ed. Stephen Buckle (Cambridge University Press, 2007), 25.

113 David Hume, *A Treatise of Human Nature*, 1739, ed. L.A. Selby-Bigge, revised by P.H. Nidditch (Clarendon Press, 1975).

114 Hume, *An Enquiry Concerning Human Understanding*, 58.

115 Hume, *An Enquiry Concerning Human Understanding*, 58.

116 Garrath Williams, "Kant's Account of Reason," in *The Stanford Encyclopedia of Philosophy* (Summer 2009 Edition), ed. Edward N. Zalta, http://plato.stanford.edu/archives/sum2009/entries/kant-reason/.

117 Immanuel Kant, *Critique of Pure Reason*, 1781, abridged ed., Norman Kemp Smith, translator (MacMillan, 1934), 325.

118 Kant, *Critique of Pure Reason*, 325.

119 Jeff Malpas, "Hans-Georg Gadamer," in *The Stanford Encyclopedia of Philosophy* (Summer 2009 Edition), ed. Edward N. Zalta, http://plato.stanford.edu/archives/sum2009/entries/gadamer/.

120 Hans-Georg Gadamer, *Truth and Method*, 1960, 2nd ed., Joel Weinsheimer and Donald G. Marshall, translators (Continuum, 1994), 276-277.

121 Gadamer, *Truth and Method*, 277.

122 Gadamer, *Truth and Method*, 277.

123 Gadamer, *Truth and Method*, 284.

124 Gadamer, *Truth and Method*, 284.

125 Clement C.J. Webb in E. Richard Atleo, *Tsawalk: A Nuu-chah-nulth Worldview* (UBC Press, 2004) xi.

126 Atleo, *Tsawalk*, xi.

127 Brian Yazzie Burkhart, "What Coyote and Thales Can Teach Us: An Outline of American Indian Epistemology," ed. Anne Waters, *American Indian Thought: Philosophical Essays* (Blackwell, 2004), 15-16.

128 Burkhart, "What Coyote and Thales Can Teach Us," 16.

129 Burkhart, "What Coyote and Thales Can Teach Us," 16.

130 Cordova, *How It Is*, 25.

131 Cordova, *How It Is*, 25-26.

132 Burkhart, "What Coyote and Thales Can Teach Us," 17.

133 Linda Tuhiwai Smith, *Decolonizing Methodologies: Research and Indigenous Peoples* (Zed Books, 1999), 1.

134 Linda Tuhiwai Smith uses the Māori words *Kaua e mahaki*, but I have included a more contemporary phrase suggested verbally to me by Jenny Plane Te Paa (oral defense notes, February 25, 2016).

135 Smith, *Decolonizing Methodologies*, 119-120.

136 Burkhart, "What Coyote and Thales Can Teach Us," 17.

137 Burkhart, "What Coyote and Thales Can Teach Us," 17.

138 Burkhart, "What Coyote and Thales Can Teach Us," 18.

139 Burkhart, "What Coyote and Thales Can Teach Us," 20.

140 See Carmen Rae Lansdowne, "ORiginAL Voices: Eradicating the 'Fearful Asymmetry' or Power Imbalance between Indigenous and Western Thought in History and Theology," ed. Nestor Medina and Jeff Nowers, *Theology and the Crisis of Engagement: Essays on the Relationship of Theology and the Social Sciences in Honor of Lee Cormie* (Wipf and Stock, 2013), 93-109.

141 Donald L. Fixico, *The American Indian Mind in A Linear World: American Indian Studies and Traditional Knowledge* (Routledge, 2003).

142 Fixico, *The American Indian Mind*, xii.

143 Fixico refers here to truth, multiple purposes, and teaching people to learn.

144 Fixico, *The American Indian Mind,* xiii.

145 Cordova, *How It Is*, 71.

146 Burkhart, "What Coyote and Thales Can Teach Us," 25-26.

147 Anne Waters, "Language Matters: Nondiscrete Nonbinary Dualism," *American Indian Thought: Philosophical Essays*, ed. Anne Waters (Blackwell, 2004), 98-99.

148 Waters, "Language Matters," 103.

149 Calvin Helin, *Dances with Dependency: Indigenous Success through Self-Reliance* (Orca Spirit Publishing: 2006), 14-15.

150 Helin, *Dances with Dependency*, 15.

151 Waters, "Language Matters," 106.

152 Paula Gunn Allen, quoted in Waters, "Language Matters," 106.

153 Rauna Kuokkanen, *Reshaping the University: Responsibility, Indigenous Epistemes, and the Logic of the Gift* (UBC Press, 2007), 98.

154 Kuokkanen, *Reshaping the University*, 97-98.

155 Gayatri Spivak as quoted in Kuokkanen, *Reshaping the University*, 99.

156 V.F. Cordova, "Approaches to Native American Philosophy," in *American Indian Thought: Philosophical Essays*, ed. Anne Waters (Blackwell, 2004), 30.

157 Francis Anekwe Oborji, *Concepts of Mission: The Evolution of Contemporary Missiology* (Orbis Books, 2006), 134.

158 See also the entry "*missio Dei*" in *The Dictionary of the Ecumenical Movement*, ed. Nicholas Lossky et al. (WCC Publications, 1991), 687-689.

159 David J. Bosch, *Transforming Mission*, 390.

160 See J.H. Oldham, *Christianity and the Race Problem* (George H. Doran Company, 1924).

161 The Life and Work movement was concerned with the practical activities of churches. The Faith and Order movement was focused on the theologies and ecclesiologies of churches. In the early twentieth century they moved towards unity, and after World War II became the World Council of Churches.

162 Oborji, *Concepts of Mission*, 136.

163 Oborji, *Concepts of Mission*, 136.

164 Oborji, *Concepts of Mission*, 138-139.

165 Bosch, *Transforming Mission*, 390.

166 Bosch, *Transforming Mission*, 390-391.

167 Bosch, *Transforming Mission*, 392.

168 See Oborji, *Concepts of Mission*, 139, and Bosch, *Transforming Mission*, 392-393.

169 See Alexander Schmemann, *Church, World, Mission* (St. Vladimir's Seminary Press, 1979), 209-216.

170 World Council of Churches. "Mission and Evangelism: An Ecumenical Affirmation," in *You Are the Light of the World: Statements on Mission by the World Council of Churches, 1980-2005* (WCC Publications, 2005), https://www.oikoumene.org/resources/publications/you-are-the-light-of-the-world-statements-on-mission-by-the-world-council-of-churches-1980-2005.

171 See World Council of Churches, Commission on World Mission and Evangelism, "Together Towards Life: Mission and Evangelism in Changing Landscapes" (World Council of Churches, 2012), http://www.oikoumene.org/en/resources/documents/commissions/mission-and-evangelism/together-towards-life-mission-and-evangelism-in-changing-landscapes.

172 World Council of Churches, "Together Towards Life," 5.

173 World Council of Churches, "Together Towards Life," 5.

174 World Council of Churches, "Together Towards Life," 5-6.

175 J.C. Hoekendijk, *The Church Inside Out* (Westminster Press, 1964), 152-53.

176 Hoekendijk, *The Church Inside Out*, 168.

177 Hoekendijk, *The Church Inside Out*, 176.

178 Willem Saayman, "A South African Perspective on Transforming Mission," *Mission in Bold Humility: David Bosch's Work Considered*, ed. Willem Saayman and Klippies Kritzinger (Orbis Books, 1996), 43.

179 Philip L. Wickeri, "The End of Missio Dei: Secularization, Religions and the Theology of Mission," in *Mission Revisited: Between Mission History and Intercultural Theology in Honour of Pieter N. Holtrop*, ed. Volker Küster (LIT Verlag, 2011), 27-44.

180 Christopher Duraisingh, "From Church-Shaped Mission to Mission-Shaped Church," *Anglican Theological Review* 92, no. 1 (2010): 7-28.

181 Sebastian, "Interrogating *missio Dei*," 26-44.

182 Sebastian, "Interrogating *missio Dei*," 28.

183 Sebastian, "Interrogating *missio Dei*," 29-30.

184 See previously cited works by Tinker, and also Nicanor Sarmiento, *Caminos de la Teología India,* Serie: Evangelio y Culturas, 2 (Editorial Verbo Divino y Universidad Catholicos de Bolivia, 2000) and *Un Arco Iris de Voces Teológicas: La trilogía andina desde las experiencias quechua y aymara* (Editorial Itinererios y Universidad Catholicos de Bolivia, 2016). Randy Woodley (of Keetowah Cherokee descent) and the late Richard Twiss (member of the Sicangu Lakota Oyate) have written on Indigenous theology, but neither wrote specifically on the *missio Dei* so I haven't included them here.

185 Wati Longchar, "Editorial—Rethinking Mission in Asia," *The Journal of Theologies and Cultures in Asia* (The Programme for Theology and Cultures in Asia) 7 / 8 (2008/2009): i-xiii.

186 Tinker, quoted in Longchar, "Editorial," iii-iv.

187 Longchar, "Editorial," v-vii.

188 Longchar, "Editorial," x.

189 Longchar, "Editorial," x-xi.

190 George E. Tinker, *Spirit and Resistance: Political Theology and American Indian Liberation* (Fortress Press, 2004), 5.

191 John R. Franke, *Manifold Witness: The Plurality of Truth* (Abingdon Press, 2009), 136.

192 Franke, *Manifold Witness*, 136.

193 Franke, *Manifold Witness*, 19.

194 Bonhoeffer in Bosch, *Transforming Mission,* 375.

195 Bosch, *Transforming Mission*, 375.

196 See *Intercultural Theology: Approaches and Themes*, ed. Mark J. Cartledge and David Cheetham (SCM Press, 2011) as well as *Mission Revisited: Between Mission History and Intercultural Theology*, ed. Volker Küster (LIT Verlag, 2011) and Volker Küster and Robert J. Schreiter, *The Many Faces of Jesus Christ: Intercultural Christology* (Orbis Books, 2001).

197 Werner Ustorf, "Introduction," *Intercultural Theology: Approaches and Themes*, ed. Mark J. Cartledge and David Cheetham (SCM Press, 2011), 3.

198 Ann Belford Ulanov, "Practicing Reconciliation: Love and Work," *Anglican Theological Review* 89, no. 2 (2007): 233.

199 Ulanov, "Practicing Reconciliation," 244.

200 Ulanov, "Practicing Reconciliation," 244.

201 Holler, *Erotic Morality: The Role of Touch in Moral Agency.* Rutgers University Press, 2002, 92.

202 Wati Longchar, "Solidarity for Justice and Peace: An Asian Indigenous Perspective," *The Ecumenical Review* 64, no. 4 (December 2012): 469.

203 K.C. Abraham, quoted in Wati Longchar, "Solidarity for Justice and Peace," 468.

204 Kritzinger, *Mission in Creative Tension*, 41.

205 The Native Women's Association of Canada defines lateral violence as "when individuals who have endured oppression suppress feelings such as: anger, shame, and rage. Eventually these feelings manifest in behaviours such as: jealousy, resentment, blame, and bitterness; and they are directed toward their Aboriginal co-workers." See "Aboriginal Lateral Violence," https://www.nwac.ca/assets-knowledge-centre/2011-Aboriginal-Lateral-Violence.pdf. See also Calvin Helin, *Dances with Dependency.*

206 Kritzinger, *Mission in Creative Tension*, 43.

207 Kritzinger, *Mission in Creative Tension*, 41.

208 Kritzinger, *Mission in Creative Tension*, 41.

209 Kritzinger, *Mission in Creative Tension*, 45.

210 Gustavo Gutiérrez, *On Job: God-Talk and the Suffering of the Innocent*, Matthew J. O'Connell, translator (Orbis Books, 1998), xi.

211 Gutiérrez, *On Job*, xi.

212 Gutiérrez, *On Job*, xiii.

213 Freire, *Pedagogy of the Oppressed*, 84-85.

214 Freire, *Pedagogy of the Oppressed*, 85.

215 John D. Caputo, *What Would Jesus Deconstruct? The Good News of Post-Modernism for the Church* (Grand Rapids, MI: Baker Academic, 2007), 32.

216 Enrique Dussel, *Ethics of Liberation: In the Age of Globalization and Exclusion*, Eduardo Mendietta et al., translators (Duke University Press, 2013), 47.

217 Chela Sandoval, *Methodology of the Oppressed* (University of Minnesota Press, 2000), 69.

218 Marcella Althaus-Reid, *Indecent Theology: Theological Perversions in Sex, Gender and Politics* (Routledge Press, 2000).

219 Lisa Isherwood and Mark D. Jordan, eds., *Dancing Theology in Fetish Boots: Essays in Honour of Marcella Althaus-Reid* (SCM Press, 2010).

220 Isherwood, *Dancing Theology in Fetish Boots,* xv.

221 Althaus-Reid, *Indecent Theology,* 114.

222 John Caputo, *The Weakness of God: A Theology of the Event* (Indiana University Press, 2006).

223 Caputo, *The Weakness of God,* 7.

224 Caputo, *The Weakness of God,* 131.

225 Caputo, *The Weakness of God,* 132.

226 See "Native American Aid Programs," Partnership with Native Americans, http://secure.nativepartnership.org/site/PageServer?pagename=naa_progs_main.

227 Thomas King, *The Inconvenient Indian: A Curious Account of Native People in North America* (University of Minnesota Press, 2012), 65.

228 Caputo, *The Weakness of God,* 133.

229 Keller, *On the Mystery,* 159.

230 Keller, *On the Mystery,* 159.

231 Keller, *On the Mystery,* 159.

232 These terms have been used in similar ways and/or interchangeably by different scholars working on issues of race, political and economic disparity. See especially Paulo Freire, *Pedagogy of the Oppressed* (Bloomsbury Academic, 2000), Chela Sandoval, *Methodology of the Oppressed* (University of Minnesota Press, 2000), Nelson Maldonado-Torres, *Against War: Views from the Underside of Modernity* (Duke University Press, 2008), Enrique Dussel, *Ethics of Liberation: In the Age of Globalization and Exclusion* (Duke University Press, 2013) and *Politics of Liberation: A Critical Global History* (Norwich: Hymns and Ancient Moderns, 2011), Walter Mignolo, *The Darker Side of Western Modernity: Global Futures, Decolonial Options* (Duke University Press, 2011) and *The Idea of Latin America* (Blackwell, 2005), Mark Lewis Taylor, *The Executed God: The Way of The Cross in Lockdown America* (Augsburg Fortress, 2001), and Gustavo Gutiérrez, *The Essential Writings* (Fortress Press, 1996).

233 See World Council of Churches, Commission on World Mission and Evangelism, "Together Towards Life: Mission and Evangelism in Changing Landscapes" (2012), http://www.oikoumene.org/en/resources/documents/commissions/mission-and-evangelism/together-towards-life-mission-and-evangelism-in-changing-landscapes.

234 Carmen Rae Lansdowne, "ORiginAL Voices: Eradicating the 'Fearful Asymmetry' or Power Imbalance between Indigenous and Western Thought in History and Theology," ed. Nestor Medina and Jeff Nowers, *Theology and the Crisis of Engagement: Essays on the*

Relationship of Theology and the Social Sciences in Honor of Lee Cormie (Wipf and Stock, 2013), 99.

235 I owe the wording of this section heading to Nelson Maldonado-Torres.

236 Maldonado-Torres, *Against War*, 3.

237 Walter Mignolo, *The Idea of Latin America* (Blackwell, 2005), xiv.

238 Vincent J. Donovan, *Christianity Rediscovered*, 25th anniversary ed. (Orbis Books, 2003), 82.

239 Donovan, *Christianity Rediscovered*, 82.

240 Mignolo, *The Idea of Latin America*, 36.

241 Mignolo, *The Idea of Latin America*, 36.

242 Gustavo Gutiérrez, *Las Casas: In Search of the Poor of Jesus Christ* (Orbis Books, 1993).

243 Political choice not to separate the continent along arbitrary lines. See Mignolo, *The Idea of Latin America*.

244 See Helin, *Dances with Dependency*, 125.

245 See West, *Race Matters*, 23.

246 By anachronistic "tribal" practices I mean, for instance, when the Makah Tribe on the Olympic Peninsula of what is now Washington State resumed whale hunting in 1999, critics argued they should not be allowed to use modern technology. That an "authentic" Indigenous resumption of cultural practices necessitated a reversion to anything pre-contact, as if we didn't evolve in our technologies prior to contact with Europeans.

247 Gutiérrez, *Las Casas*, 3.

248 Gutiérrez, *A Theology of Liberation*, 20.

249 Helin, *Dances with Dependency*, 165.

250 Althaus-Reid, *Indecent Theology*, 11.

251 Althaus-Reid, *Indecent Theology*, 11.

252 Lee Maracle, *Daughters Are Forever* (Raincoast Books, 2002), 24.

253 Gutiérrez, *Las Casas*, 4.

254 Gutiérrez, *Las Casas*, 7.

255 Elisabeth Schüssler Fiorenza, *Wisdom Ways: Introducing Feminist Biblical Interpretation* (Orbis Books, 2001), 135.

256 Scholars working on liberation and liberative theologies include Thia Cooper, Santiago Slabodsky, Nestor Medina, Ivan Petrella, Jenny Plane Te Paa, George Tinker, Wati Longchar, Mitri Raheb, Emily Townes, and Joerg Rieger, to name the most recently active in the American Academy of Religion.

257 The United Church of Canada, "Defining Multicultural, Cross-cultural, and Intercultural," 2011, http://www.united-church.ca/files/intercultural/multicultural-crosscultural-intercultural.pdf.

258 The United Church of Canada, "Defining Multicultural, Cross-cultural, and

Intercultural."

259 The United Church of Canada, "Defining Multicultural, Cross-cultural, and Intercultural."

260 The United Church of Canada, "Defining Multicultural, Cross-cultural, and Intercultural."

261 Stone, Laura and Kristy Kirkup, *The Globe and Mail*. "Ottawa to spend $1.2-billion on hospital for First Nations in Northern Ontario," June 17, 2024, https://www.theglobeandmail.com/politics/article-ottawa-funding-first-nations-hospital-northern-ontario/#comments.

262 Stone and Kirkup, "Ottawa to spend $1.2-billion."

263 Stone and Kirkup, "Ottawa to spend $1.2-billion."

264 Stone and Kirkup, "Ottawa to spend $1.2-billion."

265 Alfred, *Peace, Power and Righteousness*, 126-127.

266 Alfred, *Peace, Power and Righteousness*, 127.

267 Cordova, *How It Is*, 52.

268 Cordova, *How It Is*, 53.

269 Julie Cruikshank, *The Social Life of Stories: Narrative and Knowledge in the Yukon Territory* (University of Nebraska Press, 2001), xii-xiii.

270 The *Dictionary of Mission* explains that "The concept of 'intercultural theology' does not mean first and foremost a program aiming at a universal transcultural theology. It means, rather, a method which addresses forms of expression of the eternal message of the gospel . . . that are different from those grown out of one's own intellectual, liturgical, socio-ethical, pastoral, mystical, and political culture." See Richard Friedly, "Intercultural Theology," in *Dictionary of Mission: Theology, History, Perspectives*, ed. Karl Müller, Theo Sundermeier, Stephen B. Bevans, Richard H. Bliese (Wipf and Stock, 2006), 220.

271 The United Church of Canada, "Vision for Being an Intercultural Church," https://united-church.ca/community-and-faith/being-community/intercultural-ministries/vision-becoming-intercultural-church.

272 Inculturation refers to the insertion of Christianity into a cultural context, and acculturation refers to when an individual must receive that which is foreign.

273 Freire, *Pedagogy of the Oppressed*, 69.

274 Küster, "Why Intercultural Theology is a Must," 176.

275 Reinhold Neibuhr, *Moral Man and Immoral Society: A Study in Ethics and Politics* (SCM Press, 1963), 117-118.

276 Patricia June Vickers, "*Ayaawx* (*Ts'msyen* ancestral law): The power of Transformation," PhD Dissertation, University of Victoria, 2008, http://dspace.library.uvic.ca/handle/1828/1299, 16-17.

277 Cordova, *How It Is*, 57-58.

278 Cordova, *How It Is*, 58.

279 Linda Tuhiwai Smith, *Decolonizing Methodologies*, 13.

280 Smith, *Decolonizing Methodologies*, 13-14.

281 Tom Flanagan, "From Reconciliation to Reparations: Exploiting a Noble Idea," The Fraser Institute, https://www.fraserinstitute.org/studies/from-reconciliation-to-reparations-exploiting-a-noble-idea.

282 As I raised in chapter one, for us to engage in intrasubjective theological dialogue with Euro-American society there must first be a resolution to outstanding political issues relating to Indigenous concerns (such as land claims, Canada and the United States' resistance to the UN Declaration on the Rights of Indigenous Peoples, language diversity and preservation, etc.). From an Indigenist perspective, the political is inseparable from the theological.

283 Amartya Sen, *Development as Freedom* (Anchor, 1999), 96.

284 Catherine Keller, *On the Mystery*, 36.

285 Cordova, *How It Is,* 63.

286 Cordova, *How It Is,* 63.

287 Steve Heinrichs, "An Indigenous Intrusion Troubles the House: A Call to Decolonization," in *Buffalo Shout, Salmon Cry: Conversations on Creation, Land Justice, and Life Together,* ed. Steve Heinrichs (Herald Press, 2003), 19.

288 Cordova, *How it Is*, 63.

289 Mark Laing, "Recovering Missional Ecclesiology in Theological Education," *International Review of Mission* 388 (April 2009): 23.

290 Tinker, *American Indian Liberation*, 3-4.

291 Joerg Rieger, "Theology and Mission Between Neocolonialism and Postcolonialism," *Mission Studies* 21, no. 2 (2004): 211.

292 Joerg Rieger, "God and Power, Prophets and Native Lands," in *Theology that Matters: Ecology, Economy, and God*, ed. Darby Kathleen Ray (Fortress Press, 2006), 58-71.

293 Tinker, *American Indian Liberation*, 21.

294 Vincent J. Donovan, *Christianity Rediscovered*, 25th anniversary ed. (Orbis Books, 2003), 128.

295 Anarchic an-ethics are based on biblical "strategic reversals" where the kingdom of God acts as a counterbalance to the kingdoms of the world. See Part Two, "The Kingdom of God: Sketches of Sacred Anarchy," in Caputo, *The Weakness of God.*

296 Caputo, *The Weakness of* God, 137.

297 Caputo, *The Weakness of God*, 138.

298 The doctrine of discovery resulted from fifteenth-century Papal bulls that allowed for any lands discovered without Christian inhabitants to be claimed by explorers under public international law, and was used by the US Supreme Court in several nineteenth-century

decisions that invalidated or ignored Indigenous land title rights in the US.

299 Caputo, *The Weakness of God,* 138.

300 King, *The Inconvenient Indian*, 3.

301 King, *The Inconvenient Indian*, 3.

302 King, *The Inconvenient Indian*, 215.

303 King, *The Inconvenient Indian*, 215-216.

304 See Lipsitz, *The Possessive Investment in Whiteness: How White People Profit from Identity Politics.*

305 Paul Tillich, *Love, Power and Justice: Ontological Analyses and Ethical Applications* (Oxford University Press, 1954), 67.

306 Tillich, *Love, Power and Justice*, 67.

307 Taiaiake Alfred, *Peace, Power and Righteousness: An Indigenous Manifesto* (Oxford University Press, 1999), 42.

308 Alfred, *Peace, Power and Righteousness*, 42.

309 Alfred, *Peace, Power and Righteousness*, 42.

310 Alfred, *Peace, Power and Righteousness*, 43.

311 Rita Nakashima Brock, *Journeys by Heart: A Christology of Erotic Power* (Crossroad, 1988/2000), 52.

312 Chela Sandoval, *Methodology of the Oppressed*, Theory Out of Bounds Series, vol. 18 (University of Minnesota Press, 1991), 59.

313 See Spivak's now famous article "Can the Subaltern Speak? Speculations on Widow Sacrifice," *Wedge* 7/8 (1985): 120-130.

314 Cherríe Moraga, quoted in Sandoval, *Methodology of the Oppressed*, 59.

315 Rigoberta Menchú Tum is a Maya-Quiché woman from Guatemala who won the 1992 Nobel Peace Prize for her activism on Indigenous rights in Guatemala following the armed conflicts of 1960-1996.

316 Enrique Dussel, *Ethics of Liberation: In the Age of Globalization and Exclusion*, Eduardo Mendieta, et al., translators (Duke University Press, 2013), 373.

317 Dussel, *Ethics of Liberation*, 373.

318 Dussel, *Ethics of Liberation*, 374.

319 Dussel, *Ethics of Liberation*, 374-375.

320 Karl Marx quoted in Dussel, *Ethics of Liberation*, 398.

321 Sandoval, *Methodology of the Oppressed*, 136.

322 Zygmunt Bauman, *Liquid Modernity* (Polity Press, 2000), 22-23.

323 Bauman, *Liquid Modernity*, 23.

324 Sandoval, *Methodology of the Oppressed,* 174.

325 Sandoval, *Methodology of the Oppressed,* 176.

326 John D. Caputo, *What Would Jesus Deconstruct? The Good News of Postmodernism for the*

Church (Baker Academic Press, 2007).

327 John R. Franke, *Manifold Witness: The Plurality of Truth* (Abingdon Press, 2009).

328 John R. Franke, *Manifold Witness*, 137.

329 Vine Deloria Jr., "Philosophy and the Tribal Peoples," in *American Indian Thought: Philosophical Essays* (Blackwell, 2004), 4.

330 Thia Cooper, in Enrique Dussel, *Politics of Liberation: A Critical World History* (SCM Press, 2011), xiii.

331 Ivan Petrella, in Dussel, *Politics of Liberation*, xi.

332 Petrella in Dussel, *Politics of Liberation*, xi.

333 I am intentional in my use of the word equitable here instead of equal. Indigenous Peoples have inherent rights, title, and obligations as the First Peoples of North America. We also require reparations for the irreparable harms caused to our lands and our people by colonialism.

Bibliography

Alfred, Taiaiake. *Peace, Power and Righteousness: An Indigenous Manifesto*. Oxford University Press, 1999.

Althaus-Reid, Marcella. *Indecent Theology: Theological Perversions in Sex, Gender and Politics*. Routledge, 2000.

Ashcroft, Bill, Gareth Griffiths, and Helen Tiffin, eds. *Post-Colonial Studies: The Key Concepts*. Routledge, 2000.

Atleo, E. Richard. *Tsawalk: A Nuu-chah-nulth Worldview*. UBC Press, 2004.

Bauman, Zygmunt. *Liquid Modernity*. Polity Press, 2000.

Beavon, Dan, and Jerry White. "Introduction." In *Aboriginal Well-being: Canada's Continuing Challenge*, edited by Jerry White, Dan Beavon, and Nicholas Spence. Thompson Educational Publishing, 2007.

Behar, Ruth. *The Vulnerable Observer: Anthropology that Breaks Your Heart*. Beacon Press, 1996.

Biden, Joe. Transcript of Speech. "Biden Issues 'Long Overdue' Apology for Federal Indigenous Boarding Schools." PBS News Hour. Oct. 25, 2024. https://www.pbs.org/newshour/show/biden-issues-long-overdue-apology-for-federal-indigenous-boarding-schools.

Bosch, David J. *Transforming Mission: Paradigm Shifts in Theology of Mission*. Orbis Books, 1991.

Brock, Rita Nakashima, and Rebecca Parker. *Of Proverbs and Ashes. Violence and Redemptive Suffering and the Search for What Saves Us*. Beacon Press, 2002.

Brock, Rita Nakashima. *Journeys by Heart: A Christology of Erotic Power*. Crossroad, 1988.

Budden, Chris. "The Necessity of a Second People's Theology in Australia." In *Contextual Theology for the Twenty-First Century*, edited by Stephen B. Bevans and Katalina Tahaafe-Williams. Pickwick Publications, 2011.

Burkhart, Brian Yazzie. "What Coyote and Thales Can Teach Us: An Outline of American Indian Epistemology." In *American Indian Thought: Philosophical Essays*, edited by Anne Waters. Blackwell, 2004.

Byrd, Jodi A. *The Transit of Empire: Indigenous Critiques of Colonialism*. University of Minnesota Press, 2011.

Canada, Indigenous Services Canada. "Annual Report to Parliament 2020." https://www.sac-isc.gc.ca/eng/1602010609492/1602010631711.

Canada, Parliamentary Research Branch. "Some Major Findings of the Report [Royal Commission on Aboriginal Peoples]." www.publications.gc.ca/Pilot/LoPBdP/EB/prb9924-e.htm.

Canada, Royal Commission on Aboriginal Peoples. *Report of the Royal Commission on Aboriginal Peoples, Volume 1: Looking Forward, Looking Back.* http://central.bac-lac.gc.ca/.redirect?app=rcap&id=400&lang=eng.

Canada, Royal Commission on Aboriginal Peoples. *Report of the Royal Commission on Aboriginal Peoples, Volume 5: Renewal: A Twenty-Year Commitment.* Minister of Supply and Services Canada, 1996.

Caputo, John D. *The Weakness of God: A Theology of the Event.* Indiana University Press, 2006.

Caputo, John D. *What Would Jesus Deconstruct? The Good News of Post-Modernism for the Church.* Baker Academic, 2007.

Carriero, John. *Between Two Worlds: A Reading of Descartes' Meditations.* Princeton University Press, 2009.

Cartledge, Mark J., and David Cheetham, eds. *Intercultural Theology: Approaches and Themes.* SCM Press, 2011.

Churchill, Ward. *A Little Matter of Genocide: Holocaust and Denial in the Americas 1492 to the Present.* City Lights Books, 1997.

Cordova, V.F. "Approaches to Native American Philosophy." In *American Indian Thought: Philosophical Essays*, edited by Anne Waters. Blackwell, 2004.

Cordova, V.F. *How It Is: The Native American Philosophy of V. F. Cordova*, edited by Kathleen Dean Moore et al. University of Arizona Press, 2007.

Cruikshank, Julie. *The Social Life of Stories: Narrative and Knowledge in the Yukon Territory,* University of Nebraska Press, 2001.

Deloria, Vine, Jr. "Philosophy and the Tribal Peoples." In *American Indian Thought: Philosophical Essays*, edited by Anne Waters. Blackwell, 2004.

Descartes, René. *Meditations.* 1641. Translated by John Veitch. 1901. Cosimo Books, 2008.

Dictionary of the Ecumenical Movement. Edited by Nicholas Lossky et al. WCC Publications, 1991.

DiNovo, Cheri. *Que(e)rying Evangelism: Growing the Church from the Outside In.* Pilgrim Press, 2005.

Donovan, Vincent J. *Christianity Rediscovered*, 25th anniversary edition. Orbis Books, 2003.

Duraisingh, Christopher. "From Church-Shaped Mission to Mission-Shaped Church." *The Anglican Theological Review* 92, no. 1 (winter 2010): 7-28.

Duran, Eduardo, and Bonnie Duran. *Native American Postcolonial Psychology.* State University of New York Press, 1995.

Dussel, Enrique. *Ethics of Liberation: In the Age of Globalization and Exclusion*, translated by Eduardo Mendieta et al. Duke University Press, 2013.

Dussel, Enrique. *Politics of Liberation: A Critical World History*, translated by Thia Cooper. Reclaiming Liberation Theology Series. SCM Press, 2011.

Ellis, Carolyn. *The Ethnographic I: A Methodological Novel about Autoethnography*. Altamira Press, 2004.

Fixico, Donald L. *The American Indian Mind in A Linear World: American Indian Studies and Traditional Knowledge*. Routledge, 2003.

Flanagan, Tom. "From Reconciliation to Reparations: Exploiting a Noble Idea." Fraser Institute. May 26, 2023. https://www.fraserinstitute.org/studies/from-reconciliation-to-reparations-exploiting-a-noble-idea.

Flanagan, Tom. *First Nations? Second Thoughts*. McGill-Queen's University Press, 2000.

Franke, John R. *Manifold Witness: The Plurality of Truth*. Abingdon Press, 2009.

Freire, Paulo. *Pedagogy of the Oppressed*. Continuum, 2003.

Friedly, Richard. "Intercultural Theology." *Dictionary of Mission: Theology, History, Perspectives*, edited by Karl Müller, et al. Wipf and Stock, 2006.

Gadamer, Hans-Georg. *Truth and Method*. 1960. 2nd ed. Translated by Joel Weinsheimer and Donald G. Marshall. Continuum, 1994.

Greco, John. "Introduction: What is Epistemology?" *The Blackwell Guide to Epistemology*, edited by John Greco and Ernest Sosa. Blackwell, 1999.

Gutiérrez, Gustavo. *A Theology of Liberation: History, Politics and Salvation*. 15th Anniversary Edition. Orbis Books 1988.

Gutiérrez, Gustavo. *Las Casas: In Search of the Poor of Jesus Christ*. Orbis Books, 1993.

Gutiérrez, Gustavo. *On Job: God-Talk and the Suffering of the Innocent*, translated by Matthew J. O'Connell. Orbis Books, 1998.

Gutiérrez, Gustavo. *The Essential Writings*. Fortress Press, 1996.

Harnett, Daniel. "Remembering the Poor: An Interview with Gustavo Gutierrez." *America: The National Catholic Review*, online edition, February 3, 2003. https://www.americamagazine.org/faith/2003/02/03/remembering-poor-interview-gustavo gutierrez.

Havea, Jione. "The Cons of Contextuality . . . Kontextuality." *Contextual Theology for the Twenty-First Century*, edited by Stephen B. Bevans and Katalina Tahaafe-Williams. Pickwick Publications, 2011.

Heiltsuk Tribal Council. "Haíłzaqv / Heiltsuk Meaning." https://heiltsuknation.ca/our-path-to-true-reconciliation/.

Heinrichs, Steve. "An Indigenous Intrusion Troubles the House: A Call to Decolonization." In *Buffalo Shout, Salmon Cry: Conversations on Creation, Land Justice, and Life Together*, edited by Steve Heinrichs. Herald Press, 2003.

Helin, Calvin. *Dances with Dependency: Indigenous Success through Self-Reliance.* Orca Spirit Publishing, 2006.

Hoekendijk, J.C. *The Church Inside Out.* Westminster Press, 1964.

Holler, Linda. *Erotic Morality: The Role of Touch in Moral Agency.* Rutgers University Press, 2002.

Hume, David. *A Treatise of Human Nature.* 1739. 2nd ed. Edited by L.A. Selby-Bigge, revised by P.H. Nidditch. Clarendon Press, 1978.

Hume, David. *An Enquiry Concerning Human Understanding.* 1748. Edited by Stephen Buckle. Cambridge University Press, 2007.

Isasi-Díaz, Ada María, and Eduardo Mendieta, eds. *Decolonizing Epistemologies: Latino/a Theology and Philosophy.* Fordham University Press, 2012.

Isasi-Díaz, Ada María, and Eduardo Mendieta. "Introduction: Freeing Subjugated Knowledge." In *Decolonizing Epistemologies: Latino/a Theology and Philosophy,* edited by Ada María Isasi-Díaz and Eduardo Mendieta. Fordham University Press, 2012.

Isherwood, Lisa, and Mark D. Jordan, eds. *Dancing Theology in Fetish Boots: Essays in Honour of Marcella Althaus-Reid.* SCM Press, 2010.

Kant, Immanuel. *Critique of Pure Reason.* 1781. Abridged ed. Translated by Norman Kemp Smith. MacMillan, 1934.

Keller, Catherine, Michael Nausner, and Mayra Rivera, eds. *Postcolonial Theologies: Divinity and Empire.* Chalice Press, 2004.

Keller, Catherine. *On the Mystery: Discerning Divinity in Process.* Fortress Press, 2008.

King, Thomas. *The Inconvenient Indian: A Curious Account of Native People in North America.* University of Minnesota Press, 2012.

Klein, Julie Thompson. *Interdisciplinarity: History, Theory and Practice.* Wayne State University Press, 1990.

Kuokkanen, Rauna. *Reshaping the University: Responsibility, Indigenous Epistemes, and the Logic of the Gift.* UBC Press, 2007.

Küster, Volker, and Robert J. Schreiter. *The Many Faces of Jesus Christ: Intercultural Theology.* Orbis Books, 2001.

Küster, Volker, ed. *Mission Revisited: Between Mission History and Intercultural Theology.* LIT Verlag, 2011.

Laing, Mark. "Recovering Missional Ecclesiology in Theological Education." *International Review of Mission* 98, no. 1 (April 2009): 11-24.

Lansdowne, Carmen Rae. "Humble Boldness/Bold Humility: Creative Tension and Power Analysis in Postcolonial Directions for Missiology in the 21st Century." ThM thesis, Vancouver School of Theology, 2011.

Lansdowne, Carmen Rae. "ORiginAL Voices: Eradicating the 'Fearful Asymmetry' or Power Imbalance between Indigenous and Western Thought in History and Theology." In *Theology and the Crisis of Engagement: Essays on the Relationship of Theology and the Social*

Sciences in Honor of Lee Cormie, edited by Nestor Medina and Jeff Nowers. Wipf and Stock, 2013.

Lipsitz, George. *The Possessive Investment in Whiteness: How White People Profit from Identity Politics*. Temple University Press, 2006.

Locke, John. *An Essay Concerning Human Understanding*. 1689. Abridged and edited by Raymond Wilburn. Dent, 1947.

Longchar, Wati. "Editorial—Rethinking Mission in Asia," *The Journal of Theologies and Cultures in Asia* (The Programme for Theology and Cultures in Asia) 7 / 8 (2008/2009): i-xiii.

Longchar, Wati. "Solidarity for Justice and Peace: An Asian Indigenous Perspective," *The Ecumenical Review* 64 no. 4 (December 2012): 463-471.

Maldonado-Torres, Nelson. *Against War: Views from the Underside of Modernity*. Duke University Press, 2008.

Malpas, Jeff. "Hans-Georg Gadamer." *The Stanford Encyclopedia of Philosophy*. Summer 2009 ed. Edited by Edward Zalta. http://plato.stanford.edu/archives/sum2009/entries/gadamer/.

Maracle, Lee. *Daughters Are Forever*. Raincoast Books, 2002.

Martin, Dale B. *Sex and the Single Savior: Gender and Sexuality in Biblical Interpretation*. Westminster John Knox Press, 2006.

Maté, Gabor. *In the Realm of Hungry Ghosts: Close Encounters with Addiction*. Vintage, 2009.

Memmi, Albert. *Decolonization and the Decolonized*. University of Minnesota Press, 2006.

Memmi, Albert. *The Colonizer and the Colonized*. Expanded ed. Beacon Press, 1991.

Mignolo, Walter. "Decolonizing Western Epistemology/Building Decolonial Epistemologies." In *Decolonizing Epistemologies: Latino/a Theology and Philosophy*, edited by Ada María Isasi-Díaz and Eduardo Mendieta. Fordham University Press, 2012.

Mignolo, Walter. *The Darker Side of Western Modernity: Global Futures, Decolonial Options*. Duke University Press, 2011.

Mignolo, Walter. *The Idea of Latin America*. Blackwell, 2005.

National Institutes of Health. "NIH Style Guide." https://www.nih.gov/nih-style-guide/race-national-origin.

Native Women's Association of Canada. "Aboriginal Lateral Violence." https://www.nwac.ca/assets-knowledge-centre/2011-Aboriginal-Lateral-Violence.pdf.

Neibuhr, Reinhold. *Moral Man and Immoral Society: A Study in Ethics and Politics*. SCM Press, 1963.

Neill, Stephen. *A History of Christian Missions*. Penguin, 1990.

Oborji, Francis Anekwe. *Concepts of Mission: The Evolution of Contemporary Missiology*. Orbis Books, 2006.

Oldham, J.H. *Christianity and the Race Problem*. George H. Doran Company, 1924.

Partnership with Native Americans. "Native American Aid Programs." http://secure.nativepartnership.org/site/PageServer?pagename=naa_progs_main.

Parvey, Constance F. *The Community of Women and Men in the Church: A Report of the World Council of Churches' Conference, Sheffield, England, 1981.* Fortress Press, 1983.

Reid, Michelle. "Top 10 list: How not to respond to Indigenous experiences of racism in Canada." Rabble.ca, Sept. 4, 2013. https://rabble.ca/anti-racism/top-10-list-how-not-to-respond-to-indigenous-experiences-racism-canada/.

Rieger, Joerg. "God and Power, Prophets and Native Lands." In *Theology that Matters: Ecology, Economy, and God*, edited by Darby Kathleen Ray. Fortress Press, 2006.

Rieger, Joerg. "Theology and Mission Between Neocolonialism and Postcolonialism." *Mission Studies* 21, no. 2 (2004): 201-227.

Saayman, Willem, and J.N.J. Kritzinger, eds. *Mission in Bold Humility: David Bosch's Works Considered.* Orbis Books, 1996.

Saayman, Willem, and J.N.J. Kritzinger, eds. *Mission in Creative Tension: A Dialogue with David Bosch.* S.A. Missiological Society, 1990.

Saayman, Willem. "A South African Perspective on Transforming Mission." In *Mission in Bold Humility: David Bosch's Work Considered*, edited by Willem Saayman and J.N.J. Kritzinger. Orbis Books, 1996.

Sandoval, Chela. *Methodology of the Oppressed*, Theory Out of Bounds Series, volume 18. University of Minnesota Press, 1991.

Sarmiento, Nicanor. *Caminos de la Teología India.* Serie: Evangelio y Culturas, 2. Editorial Verbo Divino y Universidad Catholicos de Bolivia, 2000.

Sarmiento, Nicanor. *Un Arco Iris de Voces Teológicas: La trilogía andina desde las experiencias quechua y Aymara.* Editorial Itinererios y Universidad Catholicos de Bolivia, 2016.

Schmemann, Alexander. *Church, World, Mission.* St. Vladimir's Seminary Press, 1979.

Schüssler Fiorenza, Elisabeth. *Wisdom Ways: Introducing Feminist Biblical Interpretation.* Orbis Books, 2001.

Sebastian, J. Jayakiran. "Interrogating *missio Dei*: From the Mission of God towards Appreciating our Mission to God in India Today." *News of Boundless Riches: Interrogating, Comparing, and Reconstructing Mission in a Global Era*, volume 1, edited by Max L. Stackhouse and Lalsangkima Pachuau. The Indian Society for Promoting Christian Knowledge, 2007.

Sen, Amartya. *Development as Freedom.* Anchor Books, 1999.

Smith, Andrea. "Indigeneity, Settler Colonialism, White Supremacy." *Global Dialogue* 12, no. 2, (2010). http://www.worlddialogue.org/content.php?id=488.

Smith, Andrea. *Conquest: Sexual Violence and American Indian Genocide.* South End Press, 2005.

Spivak, Gayatri. "Can the Subaltern Speak?: Speculations on Widow Sacrifice." *Wedge* 7/8 (winter/spring 1985): 120-130.

Starr, Kinnie. "Rifles." *How I Learned to Run: Poetry, Illustrations & Photographs.* House of Parlance Media, 2008.

Statistics Canada. "Primary health care access among First Nations people living off reserve, Métis and Inuit, 2017 to 2020." https://www150.statcan.gc.ca/n1/pub/41-20-0002/412000022023005-eng.htm.

Stone, Laura, and Kristy Kirkup. "Ottawa to spend $1.2-billion on hospital for First Nations in northern Ontario." *The Globe and Mail*, June 17, 2024. https://www.theglobeandmail.com/politics/article-ottawa-funding-first-nations-hospital-northern-ontario/#comments.

Stringer-Holden, Bridget. "First Nations Life Expectancy Plunges." CBC British Columbia. August 21, 2024. https://www.cbc.ca/news/canada/british-columbia/first-nations-life-expectancy-plunges-by-6-years-in-b-c-report-1.7301471.

Taylor, Mark Lewis. *The Executed God: The Way of The Cross in Lockdown America*. Augsburg Fortress Press, 2001.

Te Paa, Jenny. "Contexts, Controversy, and Contradiction in Contemporary Theological Education: Who Bene 'Fits' and Who Just Simply Doesn't Fit?" In *Contextual Theology for the Twenty-First Century*, edited by Stephen B. Bevans and Katalina Tahaafe-Williams. Pickwick Publications, 2011.

Tillich, Paul. *Love, Power, and Justice: Ontological Analyses and Ethical Applications*. Oxford University Press, 1954.

Timpson, Annis May, ed. *First Nations, First Thoughts: The Impact of Indigenous Thought in Canada*. UBC Press, 2009.

Tinker, George. *American Indian Liberation: A Theology of Sovereignty*. Orbis Books, 2008.

Tinker, George. *Missionary Conquest: The Gospel and Native American Cultural Genocide*. Fortress Press, 1993.

Tinker, George. *Spirit and Resistance: Political Theology and American Indian Liberation*. Fortress Press, 2004.

Tuhiwai Smith, Linda. *Decolonizing Methodologies: Research and Indigenous Peoples*. Zed Books, 1999.

Turner, Dale. *This is Not a Peace Pipe: Towards a Critical Indigenous Philosophy*. University of Toronto Press, 2006.

Ulanov, Ann Belford. "Practicing Reconciliation: Love and Work." *Anglican Theological Review* 89, no. 2 (spring 2007): 227-46.

United Church of Canada. "Defining Multicultural, Cross-cultural, and Intercultural." 2011. http://www.united-church.ca/files/intercultural/multicultural-crosscultural-intercultural.pdf.

United Church of Canada. "The Apologies." https://united-church.ca/social-action/justice-initiatives/reconciliation-and-indigenous-justice/apologies.

United Church of Canada. "Vision for Becoming an Intercultural Church." https://united-church.ca/community-and-faith/being-community/intercultural-ministries/vision-becoming-intercultural-church.

Ustorf, Werner. "Introduction." *Intercultural Theology: Approaches and Themes*, edited by Mark J. Cartledge and David Cheetham. SCM Press, 2011.

Vatican Secretariat for Christian Unity and World Council of Churches Commission on World Mission and Evangelism Joint Working Group. "Christian Witness — Common Witness." *New Directions in Mission and Evangelization 1: Basic Statements 1974–1991*, edited by James A. Scherer and Stephen B. Bevans. Orbis Books, 1992.

Vickers, Patricia June. "*Ayaawx* (*Ts'msyen* ancestral law): The power of Transformation." PhD Dissertation, University of Victoria, 2008. http://dspace.library.uvic.ca/handle/1828/1299.

Waters, Anne, ed. *American Indian Thought: Philosophical Essays*. Blackwell, 2004.

Waters, Anne. "Language Matters: Nondiscrete Nonbinary Dualism." In *American Indian Thought: Philosophical Essays,* edited by Anne Waters. Blackwell, 2004.

Waziyatawin, Angela Wilson, and Michael Yellow Bird, eds. *For Indigenous Eyes Only: A Decolonization Handbook*. School of American Research, 2005.

West, Cornel. *Race Matters*. 2nd ed. Vintage, 2001.

White, Jerry, Dan Bevon, and Nicholas Spence. *Aboriginal Well-being: Canada's Continuing Challenge*. Thompson Educational Publishing, 2007.

Wickeri, Philip L. "The End of Missio Dei: Secularization, Religions and the Theology of Mission." In *Mission Revisited: Between Mission History and Intercultural Theology In honour of Pieter N. Holtrop*, edited by Volker Küster. LIT Verlag, 2011.

Williams, Garrath. "Kant's Account of Reason." *The Stanford Encyclopedia of Philosophy*. Summer 2009 ed. Edited by Edward Zalta. http://plato.stanford.edu/archives/sum2009/entries/kant-reason.

Williams, Raymond. *Resources of Hope*. Verso, 1989.

Wolterstorff, Nicholas. "Epistemology of Religion." *The Blackwell Guide to Epistemology*, edited by John Greco and Ernest Sosa. Blackwell, 1999.

World Council of Churches Commission on World Mission and Evangelism. "Together Towards Life: Mission and Evangelism in Changing Landscapes." World Council of Churches, 2012. https://oikoumene.org/resources/documents/together-towards-life-mission-and-evangelism-in-changing-landscapes.

World Council of Churches. "Mission and Evangelism: An Ecumenical Affirmation." *You Are the Light of the World: Statements on Mission by the World Council of Churches, 1980-2005*. WCC Publications, 2005. https://www.oikoumene.org/resources/publications/you-are-the-light-of-the-world-statements-on-mission-by-the-world-council-of-churches-1980-2005.

York, Geoffrey. *The Dispossessed: Life and Death in Native Canada*. Vintage, 1990.

Younging, Gregory. *Elements of Indigenous Style: A Guide for Writing By and About Indigenous Peoples*. 2nd ed. Lead editor, Warren Cariou. Brush Educational, 2025.

About the Author

Photo by PJ Boyd

CARMEN LANSDOWNE (she/her/elle) is a member of the Heiltsuk First Nation, and an ordained minister in The United Church of Canada. Her previous roles have included Director of Operations at environmental nonprofits in Canada and the US, Executive Director at First United Church Community Ministry Society on Vancouver's Downtown Eastside, and Moderator of The United Church of Canada. In winter 2025 she joins the faculty at Emmanuel College, Victoria University in the University of Toronto as Assistant Professor of United Church of Canada Studies. She holds a history degree from University of Victoria and both Master of Divinity and Master of Theology degrees from Vancouver School of Theology (VST). In 2016, she earned her PhD from the Graduate Theological Union in Berkeley, California.

About the Artists

PATRICIA JUNE VICKERS (cover) is a visual artist in addition to being an internationally respected leader in the field of trauma research and programming, specifically for Indigenous peoples. Her interdisciplinary doctorate from University of Victoria included research into *Ts'msyen* language (*Sm'algyax*), and the transformative aspects of ancestral law. A mother of four and grandmother to nine, and the daughter and granddaughter of the Indian

Residential School system, she values ancestral teachings and the mystery in healing. More of her artwork can be seen at www.patriciajunevickers.com.

KATIE ANDERSON (interior art) was born and raised in Winnipeg and sprouts from mixed roots with ties to St. Peters Indian Settlement, Balsam Bay, Peguis First Nation, and is a member of the Manitoba Métis Federation. She holds Bachelor of Music Education and Bachelor of Education degrees. Reconnecting and decolonizing have been at the forefront of Katie's work in both academia and artistry. Alongside education, she has a passion for digital art, songwriting, beading, and mural painting.